GIANT STEPS FOR GUITAR

A SIX STRINGER'S GUIDE TO MASTERING COLTRANE'S EPIC

To access audio visit:
www.halleonard.com/mylibrary

7319-2466-5588-9550

ISBN 978-1-4234-3009-4

HAL•LEONARD®
7777 W. BLUEMOUND RD. P.O. BOX 13819 MILWAUKEE, WI 53213

No part of this publication may be reproduced in any form or by any means without the prior written permission of the Publisher.

In Australia Contact:
Hal Leonard Australia Pty. Ltd.
4 Lentara Court
Cheltenham, Victoria, 3192 Australia
Email: ausadmin@halleonard.com.au

Copyright © 2009 by HAL LEONARD CORPORATION
International Copyright Secured   All Rights Reserved

Visit Hal Leonard Online at
www.halleonard.com

T0057335

INTRODUCTION

For decades John Coltrane's "Giant Steps" has been a certifiable rite of passage and a trial by fire for jazz players. This labyrinthine tune contains one of the most exciting and challenging chord sequences in the genre. As such, it demands considerable woodshedding and preparation of the aspiring improviser and in turn yields immense musical rewards.

In negotiating the complicated and unorthodox "Giant Steps" chord changes, improvising guitarists face a unique set of challenges—physical, technical, and intellectual—which will be addressed and reconciled in this volume. Here we will come to grips with the twists and turns of "Giant Steps," find ways to navigate its structure on the instrument and, indeed, make satisfying music within its confines.

It is crucial to state at the outset that the musical language of the performer is of paramount importance. It is vital to put your command of essential clichès, patterns, and licks to the task at hand immediately. We all have our pet phrases. They may come to us by way of John Coltrane, Charlie Parker, Sonny Rollins, Dexter Gordon, Clifford Brown, Wes Montgomery, Joe Pass, Pat Martino, or George Benson. Any and all viable components of the functional vocabulary must be considered and made available to the mastery of "Giant Steps." Moreover, it remains the ultimate responsibility of all advancing players to continue to accumulate and refine a growing stock of such figures and expressions in their personal arsenals.

This volume is the culmination of teaching "Giant Steps" for years to guitarists of all stripes. It provides the improviser with a manual and the tools to begin and master "Giant Steps." You'll find numerous useful melodic patterns and phrases, be introduced to approaches you may not have considered, and be enlightened as to the historic and harmonic dimensions of the masterwork.

Classical musicians have long practiced challenging etudes and sharpened their skills with technical pieces. "Giant Steps" has similar benefits for you, the advancing guitarist, seeking to improve technical prowess, broaden harmonic acumen, and increase powers of improvisation.

May your "Giant Steps" take you past the hurdles and lead to greater discovery.

—Wolf Marshall

ABOUT THE AUTHOR

Wolf Marshall is a guitarist-author-educator living in San Diego, California. He has worked closely with Hal Leonard publishing since 1985 and has authored the following Guitar Signature Licks books: *Best of Jazz Guitar*, *Pat Martino*, *Wes Montgomery*, *George Benson*, *Joe Pass*, *Grant Green*, *Kenny Burrell*, and *Barney Kessel*, as well as *101 Must-Know Jazz Licks* and *Stuff! Good Guitar Players Should Know*. Marshall has been a member of the UCLA Jazz Department faculty since 2007 and is a clinician for Fender Musical Instruments. Visit Wolf online at www.wolfmarshall.com.

CONTENTS

THE RECORDING

Wolf Marshall, guitars
Mark Stefani, background tracks
Courtesy of Vision Music

Recorded at Marshall Arts Music
San Diego, CA

Special thanks to Henry Johnson, Mark Stefani, Pat Martino, and Robert Parker.

Wolf Marshall plays guitars by Roger Sadowsky, Thomastik-Infeld Jazz Swing strings, and Fender amplifiers.

Follow the audio icons in the book to keep your place. The track icons are placed after the figure numbers at the top of each figure. Time notation within the audio icon indicates where in the track each example is played. Where there are two time notations, the first is the example played at regular tempo; the second is the example played at a slower speed.

TUNING NOTES

Use track #1 as a tuning reference to play along with the audio.

Track 1

A BRIEF HISTORY

"Giant Steps" wasn't created in a vacuum. In fact, several of its characteristic chord patterns had appeared before in the repertory of standard songs, show tunes, and jazz compositions prior to John Coltrane's momentous recording of 1959. However, what Trane did with his groundbreaking efforts served to consolidate and eclipse all antecedents.

"Giant Steps'" is distinguished by its atypical *3rds-related chord movement.* This sort of harmonic motion is distinctly different from the common formulae found in most jazz pieces of the era. Where did Coltrane get the idea? Many historians and jazz experts point to the bridge of "Have You Met Miss Jones," composed by Rodgers and Hart in 1937, as the precursor of 3rds-related motion in popular music. This is certainly borne out by its harmonic structure. The progression moves through the keys of B♭ major, G♭ major, and D major—each a major 3rd apart, representing a B♭ augmented triad in the big picture. The chord changes of this standard were firmly embedded in the lexicon of the jazz language by the time Coltrane became active in the genre.

Other possible 3rds-related antecedents, arguably more remote, have been noted in Dizzy Gillespie's "Con Alma," by noted Coltrane biographer Lewis Porter, in *John Coltrane: His Life and Music* (University of Michigan Press.) In Gillespie's composition an Emaj7–G#7/D#–C#m7 progression in the first phrase ultimately moves to the unrelated key of E♭ and then to D♭, a minor 3rd below E. And Brian Priestley cites the turnaround in Tad Dameron's "Lady Bird," a durable jazz piece with which Coltrane was certainly familiar. In "Lady Bird" the final two measures contain an emblematic Cmaj7–E♭maj7–A♭maj7–D♭maj7 progression leading back to C major. Moreover, these types of cycles had been in the air and well established since the 1940s. Consider the turnaround in the intro of Charlie Parker's blues piece "Parker's Mood" (1948).

Sketches of "Giant Steps" have been traced to Coltrane's developing style and found on his drawing board as early as 1956 [Bill Cole *John Coltrane.* Da Capo Press]. Coltrane's own compositions "Nita" and "Lazy Bird," of 1957, provide ample evidence of his growing interest in 3rds-related progressions. In "Nita," motion through the keys of B♭, D major, and F major is pursued in the first five measures. This pattern clearly outlines a B♭ major triad. In "Lazy Bird" the 3rds-related progression is heard in the E♭–to–G motion of measures 3–7; outlining part of an E♭ major triad. Moreover, Coltrane applied 3rds-related patterns to standards like "If There Is Someone Lovelier Than You" (1958) in the coda, and "Limehouse Blues" (1959), in which he superimposed Cm7–D♭7–G♭maj7–A7–Dmaj7–F7 changes over the F7 chord.

By the time the master take of "Giant Steps" was recorded in May 1959, Coltrane was deeply involved with 3rds-related progressions. "Countdown" (also on the Giant Steps album) is another expression of this fascination. In the year and a half that followed Coltrane used similar harmonic strategies in originals such as "Fifth House," "Exotica," "Satellite," "26–2," and "Central Park West," as well as the reappraised standards "Body and Soul" and "But Not for Me."

These pieces effectively stretched the fabric of jazz harmony like none before and moved the genre into previously unimagined territory. Had Coltrane not played another note after October 1960, his legacy would be assured for all time based on his innovations in the "Giant Steps" period.

THE MUSIC

The Origins

The musical journey that culminated in "Giant Steps" is thought to have begun in the early fifties. At this time, John Coltrane took a year off from touring with Dizzy Gillespie's band to enroll in full-time music lessons at the Granoff School in his hometown of Philadelphia, PA. There he studied with well-known theorist and guitarist Dennis Sandole. Among topics in the saxophonist's lesson plan were "3rds relationships" as well as "deceptive resolution," "chromatic root movement," "(equal) divisions of the octave," " and "other harmonic devices."

Noted jazz educator David Baker provides another piece of the puzzle. He maintains that Coltrane's interests in 3rds-related patterns arise from the diminished scale. Baker also postulates that the scale's symmetrical structure and potential for tritone chord substitution in the hard bop era would have inevitably led Coltrane to develop the sorts of progressions found in "Giant Steps."

Nicolas Slonimsky's massive tome *Thesaurus of Scales and Melodic Patterns* (1947) offers further musical revelations. Long revered as a source book among new-music theorists, modern composers, and advanced jazz musicians, the *Thesaurus* was especially popular with hard bop players in the fifties—Coltrane among them. It is known that pianist Barry Harris introduced Slonimsky's book to Coltrane in the mid-fifties. Moreover, it is documented that Coltrane soon began to incorporate some of its patterns into his music. Several acquaintances, including pianist McCoy Tyner, recall Trane working out of the *Thesaurus* regularly during the time he was exploring 3rds-related cycles.

Tenor saxophonist, educator, and author David Demsey (*John Coltrane Plays Giant Steps* [Hal Leonard]) has demonstrated how part of the "Giant Steps" progression (the second half of the form) is based directly on Slonimsky's *Ditone Progressions* (the division of an octave into three equal parts). Demsey further asserts that the second eight measures of "Giant Steps" are almost identical (though in a different key) to the melody and harmony of Pattern No. 646 on page vi of Slonimsky's introduction in the *Thesaurus of Scales and Melodic Patterns*.

The Composition

We could well subtitle this section "The Magic and Mysticism of the Numbers." There is ample evidence, considering Coltrane's own profound interest in religion and mysticism and his openness to all traditions, that a numerical system was in play when he was composing "Giant Steps." Moreover, there are in print several examples that reveal Coltrane was attaching numerical significance to musical relationships within the circle of 5ths. Two famous examples are found in Yusef Lateef's *Repository of Scales and Melodic Patterns* (Fana Music). One of these, drawn by Coltrane himself, shows an equilateral triangle within the circle of 5ths. This would represent the equal division of an octave into three parts, or the augmented triad. Clearly, in any investigation of "Giant Steps," numbers figure prominently on both the macro and micro levels.

"Giant Steps" is a 16-bar form divided in half by character. Its two-part structure is distinguished by the way the 3rds-related strategies are expressed and manipulated. These expressions are based on two procedures. Specifically, Coltrane exploited fast-moving root-position cycles in measures 1–7 and used slower harmonic rhythm (two-bar phrases) when visiting the keys of E♭ major, G major, B major, and E♭ major in measures 8–15. The latter progression is significant; it outlines an augmented triad and travels to and from key centers via ii–V–I patterns. The former progression also spells an augmented triad in a different voicing and inversion and applies only an abbreviated V–I progression to its faster moving progression.

It is useful and illuminating to note the symmetry in the "Giant Steps" chord changes. Many players have found beauty, logic, and insight—indeed purpose—by stepping back and viewing the governing augmented triad that defines the second half of the form. From this perspective, "Giant Steps" does look like a big triangle within a circle. Does that sound too esoteric, geometric, or mystical? Consider this: The augmented triad, E♭–G–B, can be named from any of its three tones and unites the 3rds-related tonal centers. There is an inherent balance in this structure. The three relationships are *symmetrical*, each separated and joined by a major 3rd. This rendered visually is what has been called "the magic triangle." (See **Fig. 1**.)

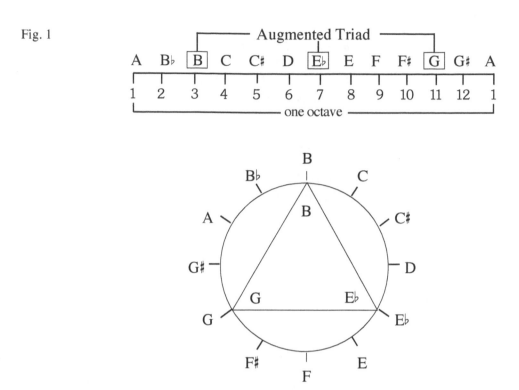

Fig. 1

The transition between the different tonal centers (points of the triangle) is made with a *ii–V* progression in and to the key of destination. (See **Fig. 2**.) For example, in going from E♭ major to G major, Coltrane used Am7–D7 to make the change. At this point further symmetry appears in the form of the *tritone*, E♭–A, an interval that divides the octave equally in half.

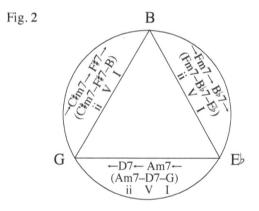

Fig. 2

Here is a basic chord chart that provides a useful view of the first eight measures of "Giant Steps." (See **Fig. 3**.) This is a more complex progression, rhythmically and harmonically. It has a faster rate of chord change and revolves around two sequentially repeated 3rds-related patterns.

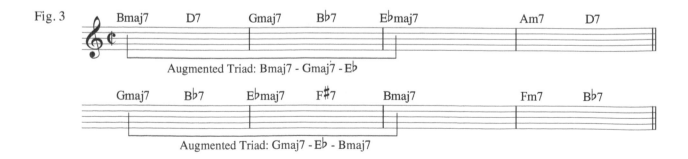

Fig. 3

The Bmaj7–D7–Gmaj7–B♭7–E♭maj7 chord changes in measures 1–3 pass through three tonal centers—B, G and E♭—at the rate of two beats per chord and suggest the greater interval spread of an "open-position" B augmented triad (B–G–E♭) or first-inversion G augmented triad. That's nine half steps dividing two octaves into three equal parts by minor 6th intervals. (See **Fig. 4**.) Minor 6ths are themselves inversions of the major 3rd interval that defines the 3rds-related conception of "Giant Steps." This expression also appears in Slonimsky's book as *Quadritone Progression* (two octaves divided into three equal parts). A ii–V progression (Am7–D7) in G, the destination key, provides motion and connection to the next phrase. When this progression is placed across two adjoining circles, it forms a larger equidistant structure.

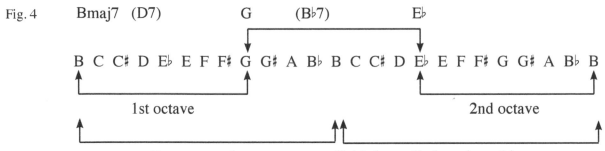

Fig. 4

B augmented = two octaves divided equally by minor 6ths

The same cycle is then repeated on different pitch levels, Gmaj7–B♭7–E♭maj7–F♯7–Bmaj7 in measures 5–8. This phrase produces a root-position G augmented triad (G–E♭–B) if perceived from the same root tone—in the second phrase, G. However, it is also an inversion of the B augmented triad starting from its raised 5th tone, G (enharmonic with F𝄪) or an inversion of the E♭ augmented triad beginning on its 3rd step. Therein lays an even larger numeric continuity. The parental B augmented triad is a central focus of the entire composition and reveals much about Coltrane's fascination with numbers, equal divisions of the octave, and symmetry.

The Improvisations

Coltrane's improvisational strategy in "Giant Steps" has been aptly described as pattern-oriented. The complex and daunting changes require considerable preparation of the performer, and it is known that Coltrane practiced the patterns heard in his solo incessantly before the recording sessions. It is an invaluable exercise for the aspiring performer to study the evolution of Trane's improvisations through the numerous alternate takes of the piece now available. This examination yields ample evidence of his considerable woodshedding.

Coltrane first recorded several takes of "Giant Steps" on March 26, 1959. The ensemble consisted of Coltrane (tenor sax), Cedar Walton (piano), Paul Chambers (bass), and Lex Humphries (drums). He returned to the studio with a different group on May 5, 1959, for the session that produced the master take and other telling alternate performances. The lineup found Trane accompanied by Tommy Flanagan (piano), Paul Chambers (bass), and Art Taylor (drums). The intervening weeks were, without doubt, periods of intense practice and preparation in which Coltrane developed and refined the content and flow of his "Giant Steps" improvisations.

"Giant Steps" is one of Coltrane's greatest "inside" solos. His adherence to melodic patterns, preconceived and practiced licks, and cadential bop formulae amounts to one of the most important and enduring improvisations of the jazz art form. It has been called an etude, a theme and variations—a thorough exploration of 3rds-related cycles in linear form. Absolutely essential to the Coltrane improvisation approach in "Giant Steps" are a handful of definitive patterns, which are exploited in myriad forms in his solos.

Coltrane was systematic. He favored a particular melodic figure to define many of the changes in the progression. This solution was a four-note pattern based on the root–2nd–3rd–5th of a major scale (steps 1–2–3–5)—for example, in B major: B–C♯–D♯–F♯. Its similarity to the major-pentatonic scale has prompted many jazz scholars and performers to dub this core figure a "pentatonic pattern." (See **Fig. 5**.)

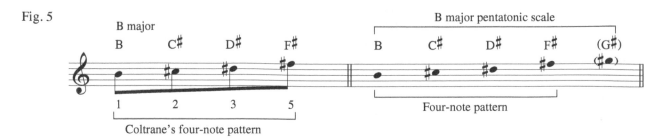

Fig. 5

There are numerous occurrences of this core figure in Coltrane's "Giant Steps" improvisations, including the use of an identical melody built on the 5th in B major: F♯–G♯–A♯–C♯ (steps 5–6–7–9). (See **Fig. 6A**.) Moreover, Coltrane routinely applied the minor-mode form of this figure to outline dominant 7th chords. For example, if he were improvising over B♭7, he would often use a descending "5th–minor 3rd–2nd–root" pattern in F minor: C–A♭–G–F (steps 9–♭7–6–5 on B♭). (See **Fig. 6B**.) This 5th substitution (F minor for B♭7) is a common procedure in modern jazz.

Also prominent in Coltrane's improvisations are simple arpeggios, both ascending and descending, particularly during the fast-moving changes in the first eight measures of the form. Coltrane used longer cadential patterns for the ii–V–I phrases in the second half of the form.

He strung these elements together and varied their application with a seemingly infinite repertory of melodic formulae and connective material—much of it indigenous to the bebop language. Through the process of motivic development and theme-and-variation, he reinvented and repurposed the use of his core patterns with each chorus.

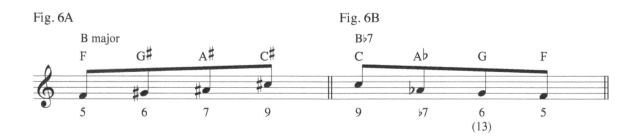

Fig. 6A   Fig. 6B

CHORDS

"Giant Steps" is arguably best understood on polyphonic instruments such as the guitar and piano, on which the progressions can be viewed, categorized, and developed from a chordal perspective. In fact, we have anecdotal information from Carl Grubbs (cousin of Coltrane's first wife, Naima) and saxophonist Wayne Shorter that John Coltrane himself practiced the changes on the piano as well as the saxophone (*John Coltrane: His Life and Music*). For a monophonic instrumentalist, such chordal drilling reaps great rewards, imbedding the harmonic sounds into the ear and consciousness.

On the guitar the rewards are even greater. Chord forms create unique visual and sonic shapes—*markers*—that serve as anchors for licks and melodic patterns, which is quite useful in single-note improvisation. Guitarists can use specific chord fingerings strategically as reference points to base, build, and contain licks for the progressions of "Giant Steps." Moreover, chord fingerings work well as tools. They tie together the unwieldy 3rds-related patterns with smooth voice leading, suggest ways to physically navigate the changes, and actually aid in keeping your place in the tune.

Preliminaries first. Consider the chord progression in the opening phrase of "Giant Steps." (See **Fig. 7**.) The changes are Bmaj7–D7–Gmaj7–B♭7–E♭maj7–Am7–D7 to G (beginning of next phrase). This 3rds-related progression is deemed to be the central harmonic pattern of the tune. It is synonymous with "Giant Steps changes."

Fig. 7   **Basic chords, first four bars**

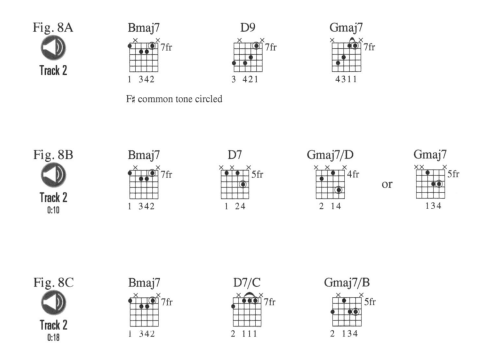

These patterns express three different fingering approaches to the first three chords of the progression.

Note the common tones in the progression. The tone F♯ is common to Bmaj7 (B–D♯–F♯–A♯), D7 (D–F♯–A–C), and Gmaj7 (G–B–D–F♯). Similarly, D is common to D7 (D–F♯–A–C), Gmaj7 (G–B–D–F♯), B♭7 (B♭–D–F–A♭), and E♭maj7 (E♭–G–B♭–D). Moreover, the D can be (and often is) carried forward in a ii–V–I progression into the next changes, Am7–D7–Gmaj7. There it functions as a pivot tone, providing a pitch that exists in both unrelated keys, E♭ and G major, and facilitates modulation. The Am7 in this case is considered an enriched Am11 (A–C–E–G–B–D) or Am7(add4) (A–C–E–G–D) chord. The D tone unites Am11–D7–Gmaj7–B♭7 and E♭maj7 in the second phrase. Clearly, common tones in the chords have great potential for linking and organizing the seemingly disparate harmonic and melodic material of "Giant Steps."

This progression places the D common tone in the upper voice of each chord from D7 on. (See **Fig. 9**.) It includes two rootless chords (D13/C and G$_9^6$/B) and a ♭5 substitution (A♭7♭5) for D7.

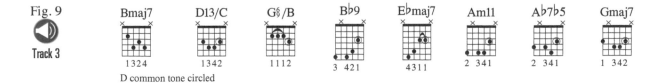

There are many ways to play the "Giant Steps" changes on the guitar. Similar progressions should be learned and played in different places on the fingerboard. The possibilities are myriad. Here are a few basic possibilities. (See **Figs. 10A–E**.) The goal is to express the progression with smooth voice leading and connective common tones. Note the free mixture of various root-position chords, extensions, inversions, and enriched altered and rootless voicings.

Fig. 10A — Track 3 0:14

Bmaj7/F#	D13/F#	Gmaj7	Bb13/Ab	Ebmaj9/G	Am9/G	D13/F#	Gmaj7

Fig. 10B — Track 3 0:28

Bmaj7	D9	Gmaj7	Bb13/Ab	Eb6/G	Am9	D13	Gmaj7

Fig. 10C — Track 3 0:42

Bmaj7	D13/C	Gmaj9/B	Bb7	Ebmaj7/Bb	Am11	D9/C	G6/B

Fig. 10D — Track 3 0:56

Bmaj9/D#	D7	Gmaj7/D	Bb13/D	Ebmaj7	Am7/E	D7b9/Eb	Gmaj7/D

Fig. 10E — Track 3 1:10

Bmaj7	D13/C	Gmaj7/B	Bb13	Eb6	Am9	D9	Gmaj7

Melodic patterns and licks from the bebop and post-bop language dovetail nicely with the chords above. In these next examples (see **Figs. 11A–B**), based on the first four measures of "Giant Steps," a chord form appears directly above its related melodic line. By performing the melodies with an awareness of and connection to their chordal counterpart, a guitar player physically, visually, and intuitively links the vital areas of single-note jazz improvisation and harmony.

Rather than a methodology, this is an *approach*—a conception or view—which harnesses the harmonic attributes of the instrument to support melody. The melody line is seen as living inside or near the chord shapes. This perspective yields a linear phrase based on the changing vertical harmonies and their interlocking physical forms.

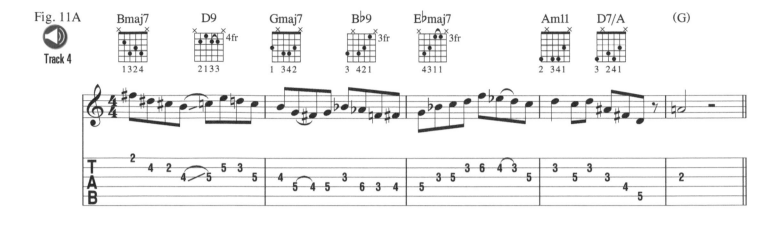

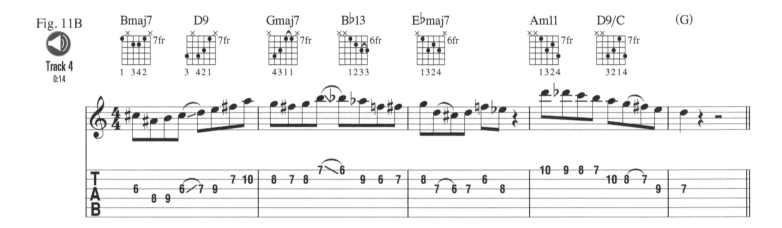

Triads and three-note partial chords offer a more utilitarian and compact solution. Using these forms as nuclear components of larger and more complex chords, the "Giant Steps" changes are accordingly viewed in partial voicings or harmonic "bites." These smaller forms are in turn endowed with greater flexibility and more potential for melodic embellishment. That means triads and partial chords are malleable and easily connected with a variety of melodic patterns and licks. And they are less subject to the harmony-specific chord tones of larger sonorities.

This phrase demonstrates the use of triads and partial chords as reference points for improvisation in the first four measures of "Giant Steps."

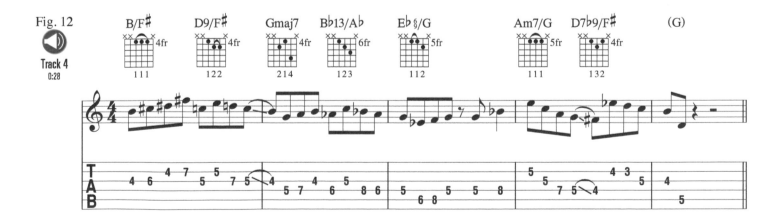

This phrase is played in a higher register and employs a combination of four- and three-note shapes as chordal reference points.

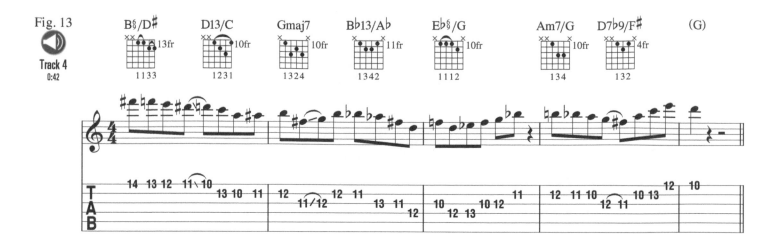

Fig. 13 · Track 4 · 0:42

Many guitarists use guide-tone shapes or "shell chords" to define a progression. These forms are particularly useful in comping. A shell chord is based on the harmonically active tones of a 7th chord in its most distilled form: the defining 3rd and 7th (the guide tones) voiced as a tritone (dominant-7th and diminished chord), or perfect 4th/5th (major and minor 7th chords) in the upper structure. The root or 5th (harmonically neutral tones) is played in the bass, generating a three-note chord which contains only the essential harmonic information.

The following examples (see **Figs. 14A–B**) present the first four-bar phrase of "Giant Steps" in shell chords. These comping progressions offer another dimension to the linking of chord shapes and melodies and should be applied to improvisation as in the above phrases.

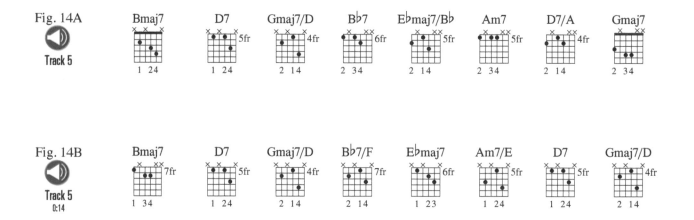

Fig. 14A · Track 5

Fig. 14B · Track 5 · 0:14

This music example (see **Fig. 15**) and audio track contains a larger guitar version of the "Giant Steps" harmony expressed as typical chord voicings and progressions. It is played over one chorus of the 16-bar form. Note the use of common tones and pivot tones as well as standard ii–V–I progressions and the substitution pattern ii–♭II–I.

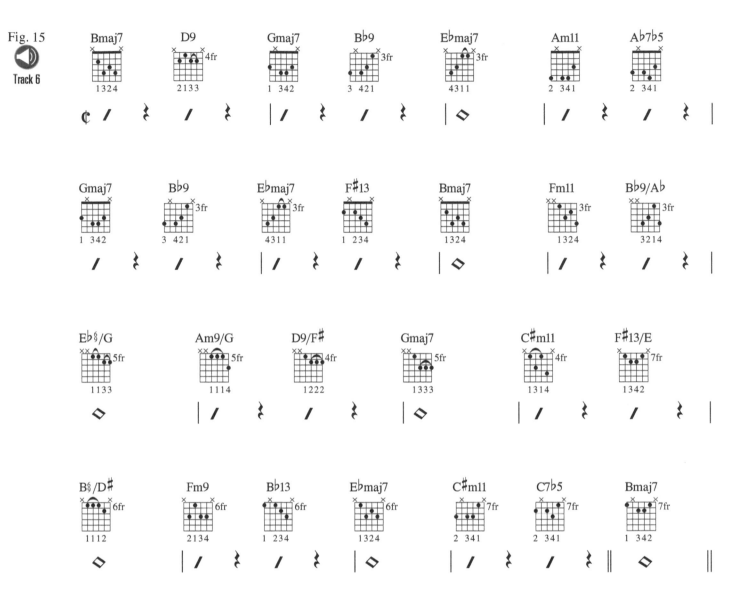

A GUITAR APPROACH TO THE MUSIC

In establishing a guitar approach to "Giant Steps" it is crucial that the aspiring player be fluent with not only the stylistic melodic patterns saxophonist John Coltrane used in his improvisations, but also with the essentials—the standard licks of the bebop language. In transferring those sax, trumpet, and other instrumental lines to the guitar, an important step in the player's development is taken and accomplished.

How and from where do we get these essentials? Music transcription remains a superb method for accomplishing the goal. Transcription has long been the proven method by which players access new material and teach themselves. Learning by ear is another term for transcription; call it "transcribing without paper."

When a player borrows from the repertory of the giants, they are going directly to the source in its purest form. And the rewards are enormous. The all-important basic elements of jazz improvisation can be acquired by transcribing, studying, and assimilating operative phrases from Charlie Parker, Clifford Brown, Sonny Rollins, Oscar Peterson, Hampton Hawes, Joe Pass, Pat Martino, or Wes Montgomery for starters.

These essentials must then be practiced, memorized, applied to your instrument and personal improvisations, and made second nature. If you're not a transcriber, you ought to be—but in any event there are now countless reliable and accurate resources available, from standard transcription and lick books to full-blown play-along products, not to mention much-improved tools for slowing down digital audio with hardware or on the computer.

Common Tones, Leading Tones, and Neighbor Notes

Absolutely central to developing a guitar approach for "Giant Steps" is the need for smooth connections and filling lines between melodic patterns. That's where specific musical devices like *common tones*, *leading tones*, and *neighbor notes* come into the picture. For example, G is a common tone uniting the tonal centers of G major and E♭ major, as in measures 5–8 of the form. It is the tonic of G major, the 13th of B♭7, and the 3rd of E♭maj7. In this example (see **Fig. 16**) the common-tone idea is emphasized with the repeated G note and slurs. Moreover, in improvisation it can be "held over" to imply the ♭9th of an altered F♯7 chord (F♯7♭9).

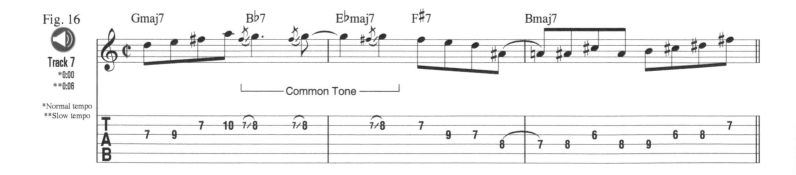

Leading-tone strategy works similarly. (See **Fig. 17**.) Imagine a B♭ tone in the key of E♭, the 5th of an E♭maj7 chord. As part of a melody it pushes upward as a leading tone to target B, the 9th of an Am7 chord. Here, it acts momentarily as the enharmonic A♯, and then begins a typical hard-bop phrase in G major from that note.

Fig. 17

Track 7
0:14
0:19

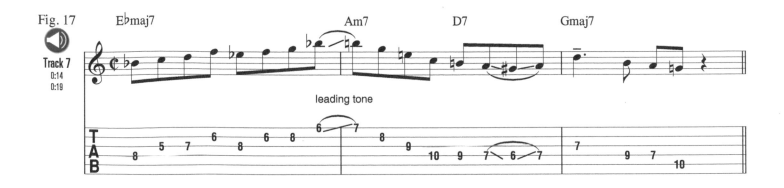

Leading-tone strategy is also used as an upper neighbor note to approach a chord tone from the opposite direction. Coltrane himself used this motion in his first solo chorus of the master take in measures 3–4. Here, a rising scale line in E♭ major reaches F and then descends to E, the 5th of Am7 in the key of G major. (See **Fig. 18**.) This phrase includes an essential voice-leading lick from the bebop language. Note the wide interval leap, encircling melody, and purposeful chromaticism to emphasize the melodic destination: the D tone in the V–I portion of the line in G.

Fig. 18

Track 7
0:27
0:32

On the guitar many melodic patterns are facilitated by visualizing their fingered shapes on the instrument. This valuable attribute can be put to good use in "Giant Steps." For example, in this phrase (see **Fig. 19**) the core motif or cell is the four-note 1–2–3–5 Coltrane pattern. It is played in varied forms and applications over the first three measures of the changes. A common fingering shape, albeit on different string sets, is shared by the figure over Bmaj7 in measure 1 (beats 1 and 2), and E♭maj7 in measure 3. The four-note ascending patterns over D7 and Gmaj7 are played with the exact same shape on different string sets.

Fig. 19

Track 7
0:40
0:45

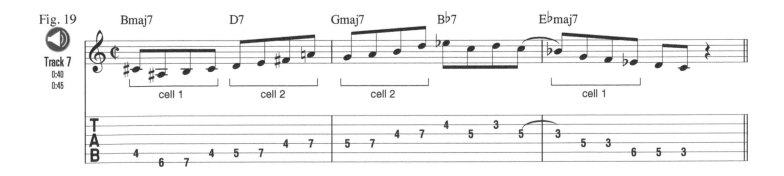

Patterns for Guitar

Most aspiring guitarists are intimidated when they first confront the "Giant Steps" changes. They are particularly confounded by the tricky fast-moving 3rds-related progressions in the first eight measures (specifically bars 1–3 and 5–7). These sections of the piece, arguably, require the most preparation and practice. The complications are exacerbated by the physical nature of the guitar itself. The question of positional playing versus linear playing—vertical versus horizontal motion, various fingering options, and plural locations of unison pitches on the fretboard—naturally arises and must be factored into an improviser's conception.

These decisions initially create great confusion and produce impediments to the formulation of a solid guitar approach. It goes without saying that strategies for attaining competence in both dimensions—positional and linear—must be developed on the guitar before unrestricted improvisation can take place. That means making the language playable all over the instrument in places where it can be accessed freely in the heat of the moment.

Positional Patterns

It is valuable at the outset to develop fluency with the core patterns of "Giant Steps" on the guitar in many different positions. We have a fingerboard of 12-plus frets—let's use them. If we take a typical phrase containing the classic Coltrane patterns through the changes in measures 1–4 and explore the playing of this melody in various positions, we have a logical starting point. Seeing and hearing these patterns all over the fretboard provides insight, builds facility, reveals possibilities, and serves as a useful introductory etude.

In the next section, **Figs. 20A–F** present a characteristic "Giant Steps" melody over the B–D7–G–Bb7–Eb–Am7–D7 changes in various positions. This is a summary of the Trane components in play in all eight examples. The prevalent 1–2–3–5 pattern is used over B and D7 and arpeggios over G and Am7. A 5–b3–2–1 pattern in F minor is applied to Bb7; this is a primary substitution in the jazz language. A scalar line marks the full measure in Eb major. Note the combination of a strict ascending partial scale on beats 1 and 2 and the 1–2–3–5 pattern, here beginning on Bb (Bb–C–D–F), on beats 3 and 4. The resolution to Am7 is accomplished with an upper-neighbor F–E approach in measures 3–4.

On the guitar it is absolutely essential to become familiar with the various positions in which this melody can be played. Moreover, depending on the desired phrasing, a player can also use a four- or three-finger fretting style or a hybrid combination of the two. You are encouraged to explore various possibilities.

16

Fig. 20C

Fig. 20D

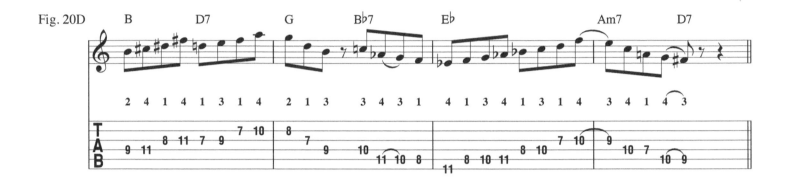

Fig. 20E

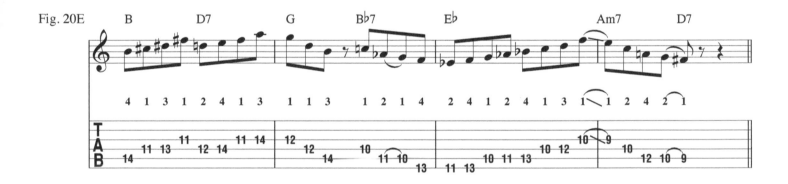

Fig. 20F

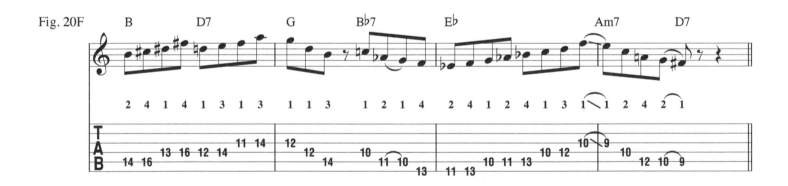

Some of these phrases will become your favorites at first; others may require more time and familiarity to develop a suitable comfort level. Bear in mind that these fingerings may be transposed and used for the second four measures of "Giant Steps" as well. Moreover, the higher-register melodies of **Figs. 21A–B** may actually be more useful when played in the seventh and ninth positions for the chord cycle of G–B♭7–E♭–F♯7–B–Fm7–B♭7. They are presented here beginning on B in the interest of completeness, to set forth a group of fingerings utilizing the entire fingerboard.

Fig. 21A offers another positional possibility as well as a change in register. Here, the melody is played an octave higher than the six previous phrases. This example completes the preliminary exploration of the fretboard and serves to introduce one more important concept, direct transposition, depicted in **Fig. 21B**. Point: The guitar is a natural transposing instrument. This example transposes the previous phrase to begin on G.

If we take the initial phrase and move it down a major third into the tenth position, we have a solution, albeit mechanical, to the next cycle, which begins on G major. See Fig. 21B. The goal is to create variations and new connections when making these sorts of transpositions. This ability increases with familiarity and practice time spent in the woodshed.

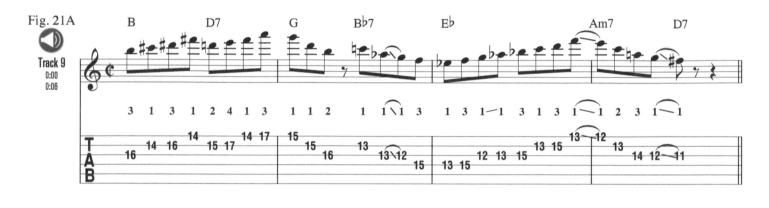

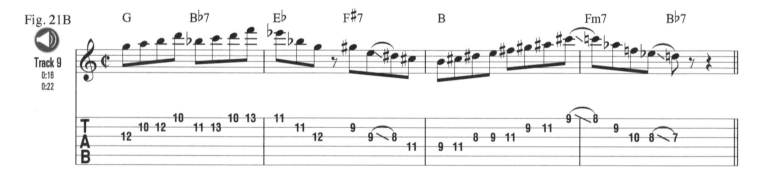

Linear Patterns

Another guitar approach to "Giant Steps" involves linear playing, or horizontal motion on the fretboard. There is simply no better way to begin than with some demonstrative phrases that embody the idea and techniques.

In navigating the tune's complex changes it is useful to have strong aural, physical, and visual reference points on the fretboard. These are even more vibrant and useful when harmonically tied to related chord forms.

In **Fig. 22**, the previous sample phrase travels in linear motion from the fourth position to the eighth and seventh positions. Note the bracketed 1–2–3–5 patterns for B and D7. These indicate identical fingerings and string groups. Notice how this phrase shifts through various forms from the positional section.

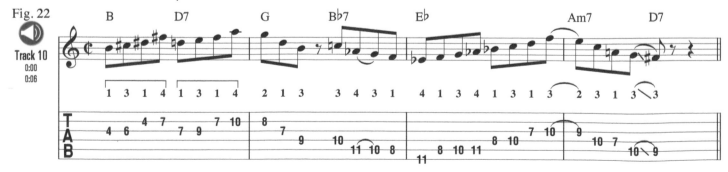

Fig. 23 takes the same phrase in different directions. It begins with linear descent and a change to a different string group. In the conclusion the phrase changes course and assumes ascending motion. The melodies, however, stay intact.

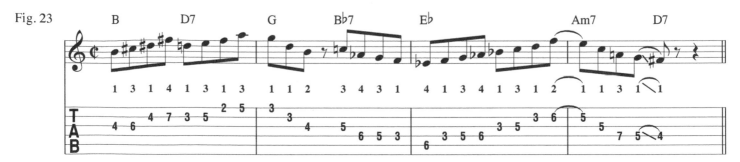

Fig. 23

Pivot points are helpful visual and physical aids on the guitar. **Figs. 24A** and **25A** present the first two measures of the sample phrase in two different linear expressions. Both veer off from the established motion of the melody line with a pivot point based on two different ii–V–I chord patterns. Related chord forms reinforce the physical connection between melodic direction and fingering possibilities. Here, a related ii-V-I progression in E♭ is suggested in 24B and 25B.

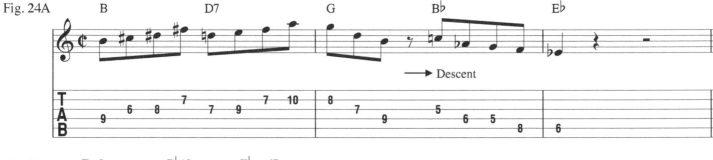

Fig. 24A

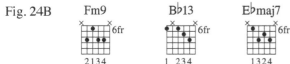

Fig. 24B

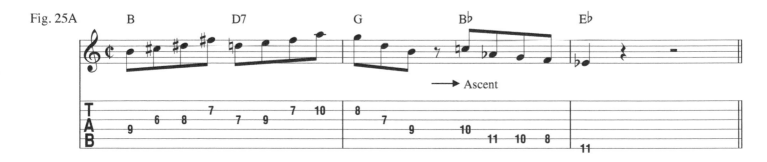

Fig. 25A

Fig. 25B

Close Pattern Motion

Chord forms are especially useful for depicting another core pattern in "Giant Steps" on the guitar. Besides 1–2–3–5 patterns, arpeggios, and partial scales, Coltrane employed what I call *close patterns*. These can be defined and codified using chord forms close to each other, often sharing common tones. (See the "Chords" chapter for more.) Consider the following phrase and its related chord shapes. Note how close the melodic shapes are to each other and the subtle half-step connective motion between patterns.

Close patterns play off tones other than the tonic like the 3rd, 5th, and 7th of the chord. **Fig 26A** is a typical phrase. Note the minimal fretboard motion. Shifts are largely confined to half-step moves, yet all the harmonic connections are made and smooth voice-leading results.

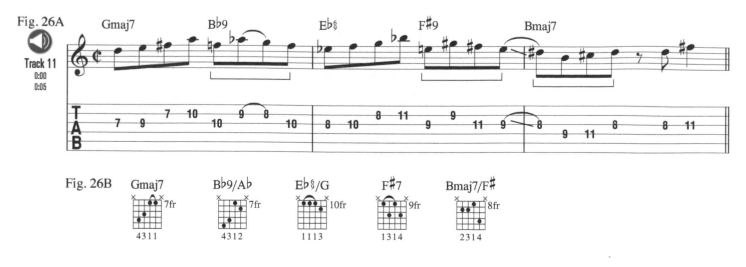

Another approach to close patterns involves using the half steps as leading tones and neighbor notes. Tight *encircling figures* or enclosing figures (targeting) are produced as a natural byproduct of this procedure. In **Fig. 27A**, note the enclosure of D by D♯ and C♯ in measure 1 (beats 2 and 3), and B♭ by B and A in measure 2 (beats 2 and 3).

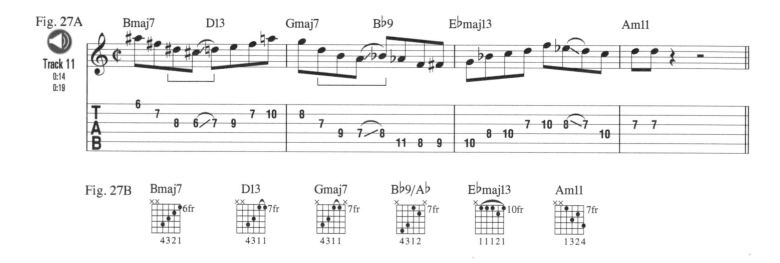

BASIC "TRANE-ING" FOR GUITAR

Before you can take "Giant Steps" you must be comfortable with baby steps. One small step toward mastery involves the application of purposeful single-note melodic patterns to the chord progression. This is the jazz guitar equivalent of Hanon etudes for classical pianists. I call it "Basic Trane-ing."

On the guitar, Basic Trane-ing requires acquisition and assimilation of the necessary patterns on two levels: (1) as melodic figures defining the changes and the chord of the moment, and (2) as physical shapes scattered in different locations on the fingerboard. The challenge for the guitarist is to develop comfort and fluency with these aspects and the patterns so that improvisations become second nature.

The following Trane-ing phrases (**Figs. 28–76**) are directed at the first four measures of the "Giant Steps" changes, arguably the most daunting section of the song form:

|| B–D7 | G–B♭7 | E♭ | Am7–D7 ||

These phrases can and should be transposed to the progression starting on G in the next four measures. They are situated in various positions and use both cycle patterns and close patterns.

Cycle Patterns typically are four-note figures. They are most often played 1–2–3–5 (root–2nd–3rd–5th steps) from the tonic of each chord outlining the chord progression's 3rds-related cycles. In Basic Trane-ing cycle patterns are also played from the 5h of a chord. For example, a G major cycle pattern can also be spelled 5–6–7–9 (D–E–F#–A).

Close Patterns involve subtler half-step motion. They are often smaller or "compressed versions" of cycle patterns. For example, the common 1–2–3–5 figure may become 3–1–2–3 as in **Fig. 30**, measure 2 (Gmaj7), **Fig. 33**, measure 1 (D7), and **Fig. 37**, measure 1 (Bmaj7). Close patterns often include *chromatic embellishments* as in **Fig. 30**, measure 2 (B♭7). They work well on the guitar physically.

Here are 49 Basic Trane-ing phrases. These four-bar examples are played in different positions on the instrument, move in different directions, have different melodic contours and goals, and combine key elements of Coltrane's pattern approach and the bebop language.

A few additional points are worth mentioning. The strict *bebop scale* (dominant 7th sound) is played in typical descending form in **Figs. 32** and **40** over Am7 and D7 in measure 4. Variants of the bebop scale are found in **Figs. 39, 52, 59,** and **76**. The bebop scale plus an augmented triad (D+) produce a genre-specific cadential figure in **Figs. 28, 36, 44, 46,** and **66**, also over the Am7–D7 change.

Most of the phrases are grouped in strings of steady eighth notes. At slower tempos, these are played with a swing feel. At faster tempos, upwards of 220, they are rendered as even eighth notes. The well-known bebop and post-bop practice of ending an eighth-note phrase on the upbeat of beat 3 occurs in **Figs. 31, 34, 38, 39, 40, 41, 43,** and **54**. A stylistic syncopated rhythmic pattern is employed in **Figs. 46, 52,** and **59**.

Several other aspects of the bebop language are included in Basic Trane-ing. A favorite *neighbor-note* pattern is played in **Fig. 28** (measure 2, Gmaj7), **Fig. 41** (measure 2, Gmaj7), **Fig. 45** (measure 2, Gmaj7), and elsewhere. The same neighbor-note pattern is applied sequentially to create a close-pattern figure in **Fig. 44** (measure 2, Gmaj7–B♭7). A major-blues lick appears in **Figs. 35** and **69** (measure 3, E♭maj7).

Minor arpeggios and complimentary diminished sounds are used to produce ii–altered V lines in **Fig. 29** (measure 4, Am7–D7), **Fig. 34** (measure 4), **Fig. 42** (measure 4), and elsewhere. The full eight-tone diminished scale (symmetric alternating half and whole steps) can also be applied to Am7–D7 as in **Figs. 45** (measures 3 and 4) and **67** (measure 4). In the course of internalizing the basic patterns, elements of the phrases will begin to overlap and suggest alternative lines—a process which is at the heart of improvised music. In order to achieve the requisite fluency and comfort—as well as the ability to think ahead of the chord of the moment—it is imperative to practice the patterns until they are fully internalized.

These 49 melodic patterns are played over the crucial first four measures of "Giant Steps" accompanied by a piano-bass-drums track. After learning and mastering these phrases, transpose them to begin on the G chord, as in the second four measures of "Giant Steps." The latter four-measure variants beginning on G are then linked to the given material (beginning on B) to form longer eight-bar statements. It is incumbent upon the player to create links once the preliminary material is comfortably under the fingers. Audio track 61 is the accompaniment minus the guitar and is designed to be used in the woodshed to practice and assimilate the patterns.

49 Basic Patterns

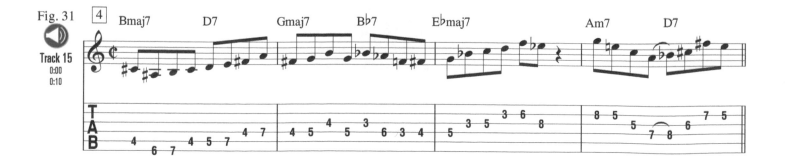

Fig. 32

Track 16
0:00
0:10

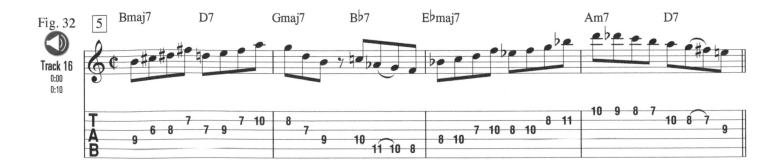

Fig. 33

Track 17
0:00
0:10

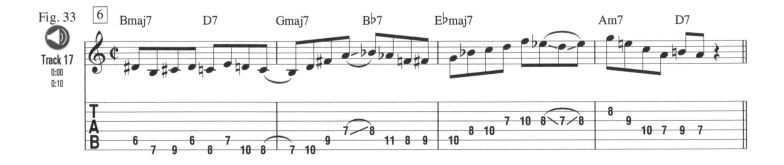

Fig. 34

Track 18
0:00
0:10

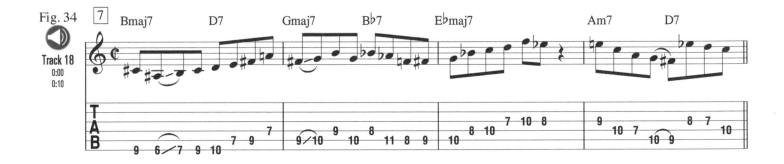

Fig. 35

Track 19
0:00
0:10

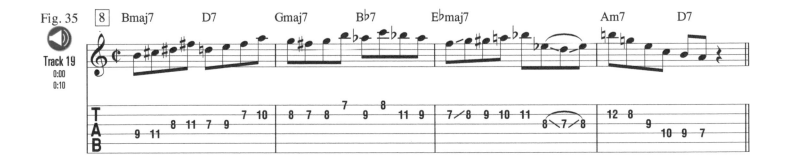

Fig. 36

Track 20
0:00
0:10

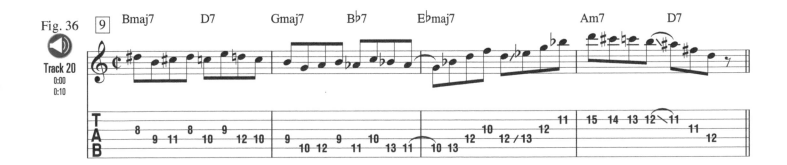

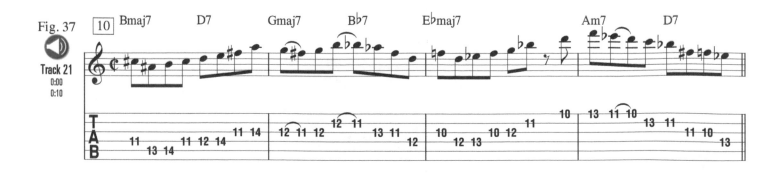

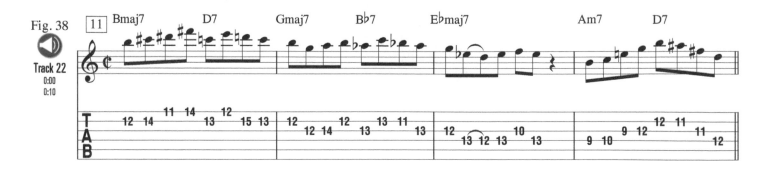

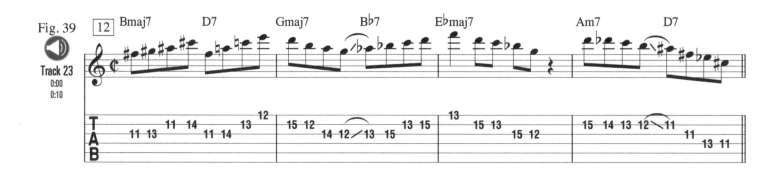

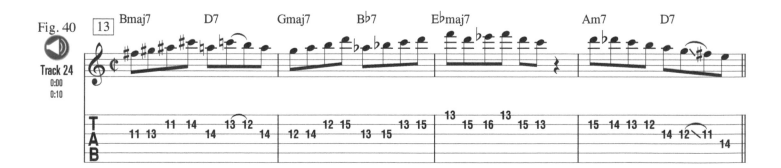

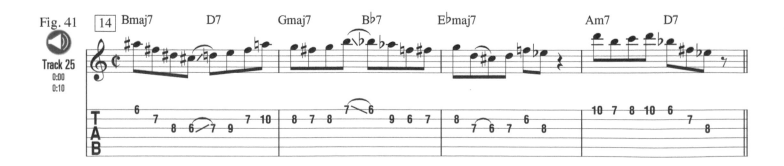

Fig. 42

Track 26
0:00
0:10

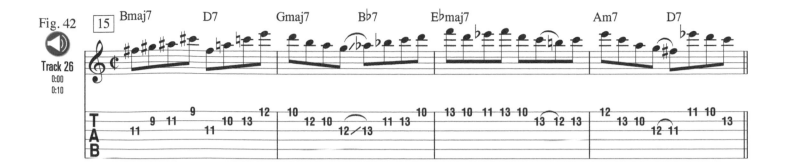

Fig. 43

Track 27
0:00
0:10

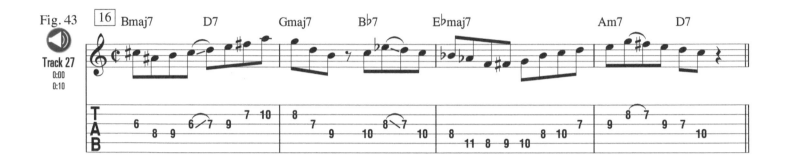

Fig. 44

Track 28
0:00
0:10

Fig. 45

Track 29
0:00
0:10

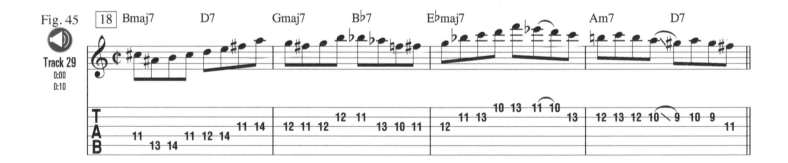

Fig. 46

Track 30
0:00
0:10

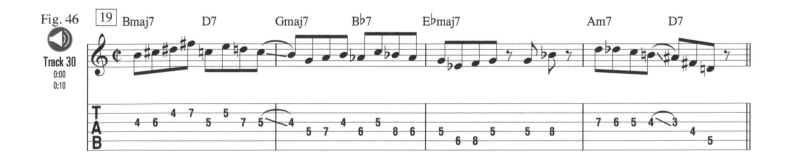

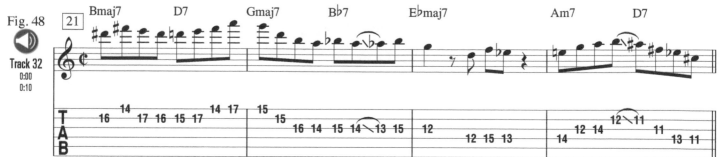

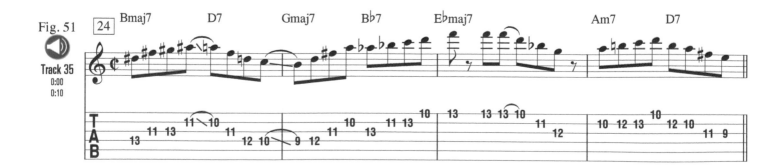

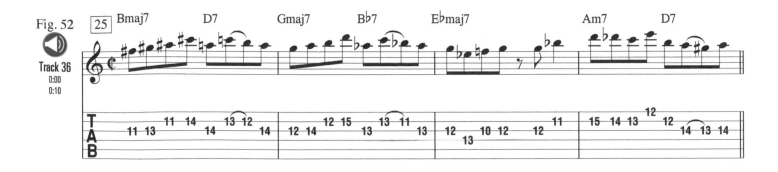

Fig. 52
Track 36
0:00
0:10

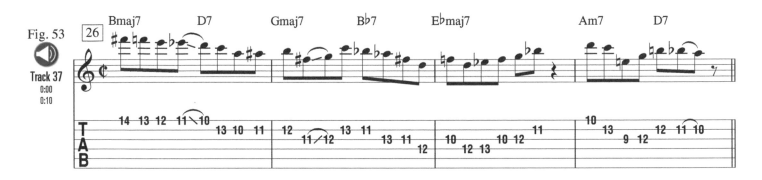

Fig. 53
Track 37
0:00
0:10

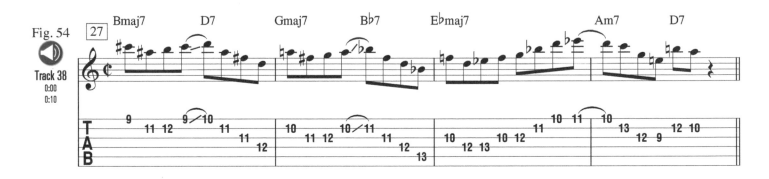

Fig. 54
Track 38
0:00
0:10

Fig. 55
Track 39
0:00
0:10

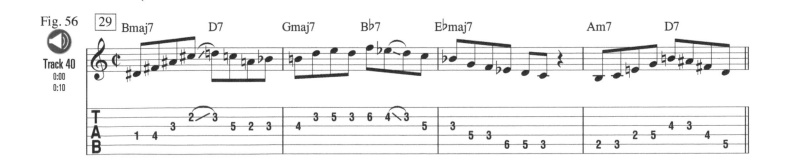

Fig. 56
Track 40
0:00
0:10

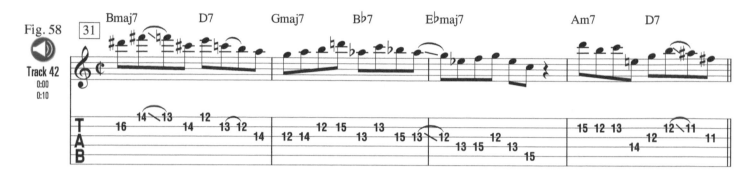

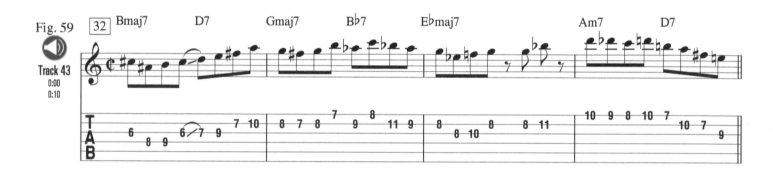

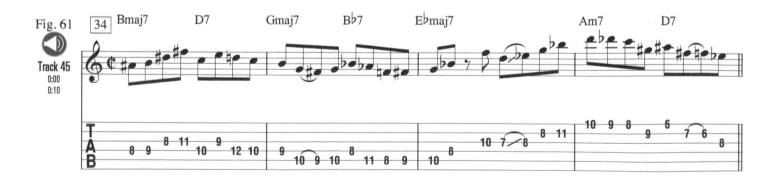

Fig. 62
Track 46
0:00
0:10

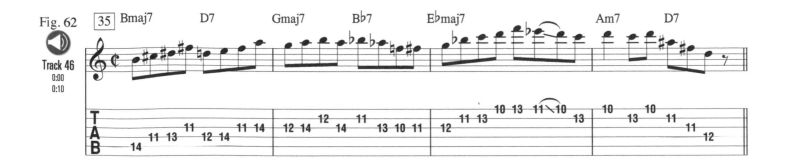

Fig. 63
Track 47
0:00
0:10

Fig. 64
Track 48
0:00
0:10

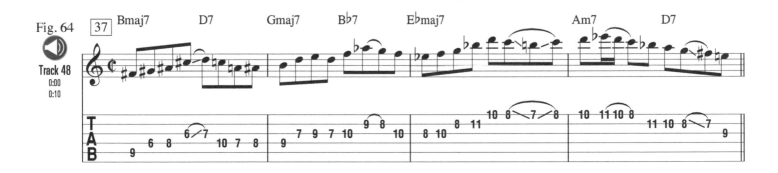

Fig. 65
Track 49
0:00
0:10

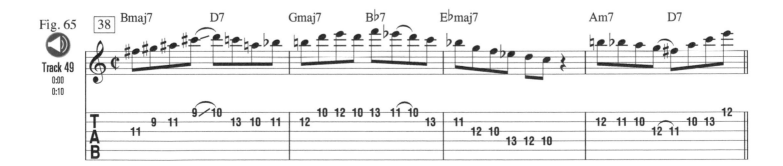

Fig. 66
Track 50
0:00
0:10

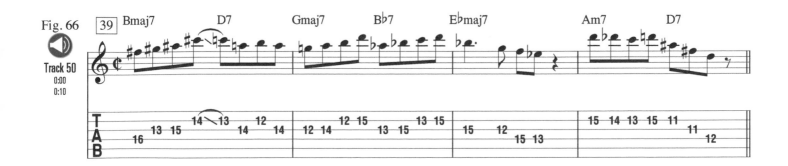

Fig. 67

Track 51
0:00
0:10

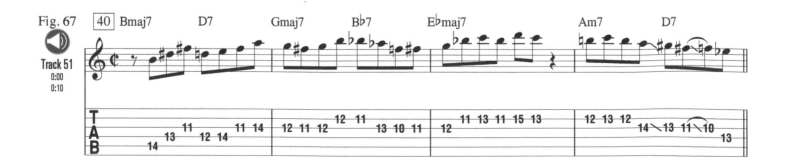

Fig. 68

Track 52
0:00
0:10

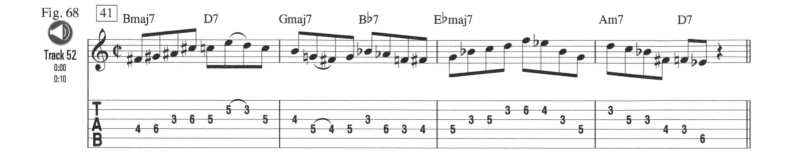

Fig. 69

Track 53
0:00
0:10

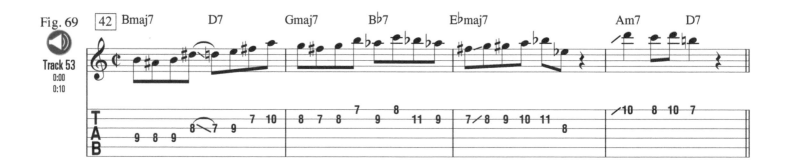

Fig. 70

Track 54
0:00
0:10

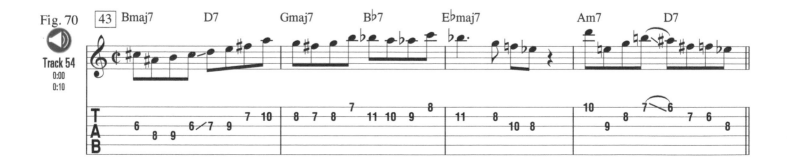

Fig. 71

Track 55
0:00
0:10

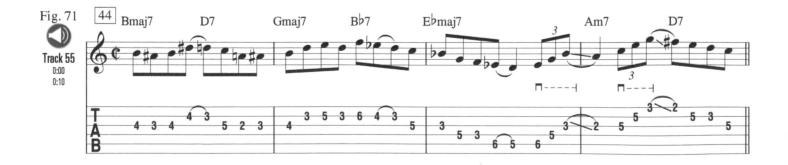

RHYTHMIC APPROACHES TO IMPROVISATION

Rhythm has always been a unifying factor in music. For many listeners, rhythm is the most readily recognized and appreciated aspect of improvisation. It resonates at the primal level of listening. That posited, how does the idea of applying rhythmic ideas relate to the complex changes of "Giant Steps?" While the idea of using rhythm as a device for improvisation may not seem as obvious or appropriate a tactic, it is a valuable and viable approach when certain preliminary concepts are understood and mastered. Moreover, the sound of rhythmic phrases can add great variety and interest to an improvisation consisting largely of melodic patterns and arpeggios.

A rhythmic approach to any music implies the subordinating of melodic material to the second tier. In a rhythmic approach to "Giant Steps," the emphasis is on rhythm and not the conventional patterns. Therein lies their potential for variety. Let's begin with the challenging first eight measures and their 3rds-related chord sequences.

One solution for tying the chords together is to employ common tones in key places. (See the "Chords" chapter for more.)

Common tones and rhythmic approaches are complimentary and synergistic. A telling illustration is offered in **Fig. 78**, based on a single common tone maintained through the first three chords of measures 1–2 and 5–6. The F♯ is a common tone that unites Bmaj7, D7, and Gmaj7. The D common tone unites Gmaj7, B♭7, and E♭maj7.

The rhythmic approach in this example exploits a sound heard in tunes like "It Don't Mean a Thing If It Ain't Got That Swing" and "One Note Samba." Here, the syncopated rhythm played on a single tone is used as a repeated two-note motif. It connects the first three chords in measures 1–2 and 5–6 and then gives way to more typical bop melodies in 3–4 and 7–8. The motif consists of two eighth notes and an eighth-note rest (space), which creates a three-beat pattern. When repeated along the quarter-note time line, the figure generates a hemiola effect: three against four, with natural displacements and shifted rhythmic accents.

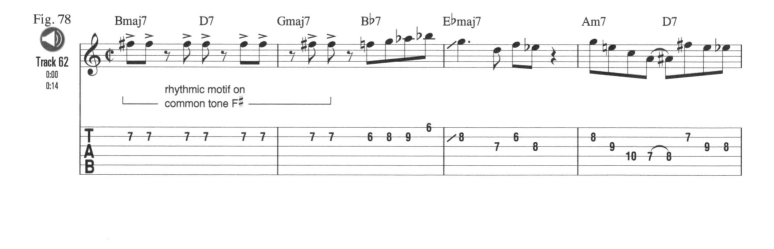

32

In this phrase (**Fig. 79**), the central rhythmic motif again exploits common tones but is a larger four-note figure with a quarter-note rest, occupying six beats. Note the textural effect of unison intervals in the first motif (F♯ common tones). The unisons are a characteristic guitar riff, toggling across adjacent strings during the common-tone pattern.

The rhythmic motif in this phrase (**Fig. 80**) is based on steady eighth notes. Note the use of a larger arpeggio shape in measures 1–2 and 5–6. The figure is rhythmically energized with a slurred articulation on the first two eighth notes of each pattern unit. The same pattern is repeated beginning on a different step in measures 5–6.

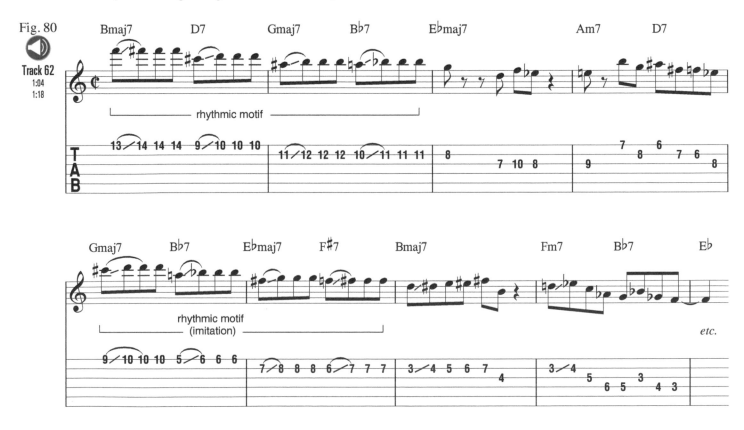

In **Fig. 81**, the previous steady eighth-note pattern is applied to a rhythmic motif of a repeated single note: the common tone B played over Bmaj7–D7–Gmaj7 changes. The B tone gives way to a dominant 7th voice-leading figure beginning on B♭ over B♭7 and a Coltrane motif over E♭ in measure 3.

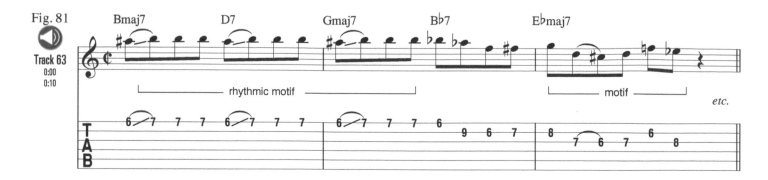

The last phrase can be further "rhythmicized" by applying the six-beat pattern of Fig. 79 to the motif and punctuating the Coltrane figure with a deliberate rest. (See **Fig. 82**.) That's the use of space to create a variation in the rhythmic domain.

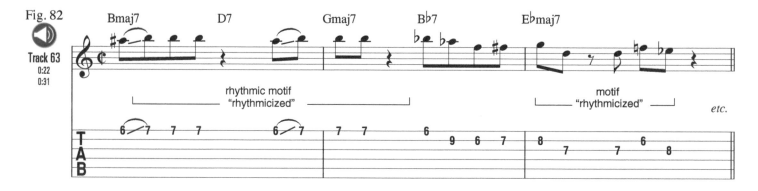

Rhythmic approaches are equally viable in the second half of "Giant Steps." **Fig. 83** harnesses the syncopation, hemiola, and shifted rhythms of Fig. 78 in a longer rhythmically-animated line over E♭maj7–Am7–D7–Gmaj7 in measures 9–12 of the form.

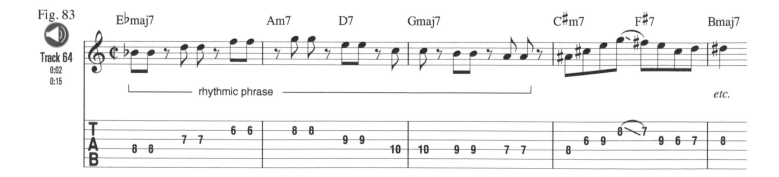

Fig. 84A, played over measures 9–12 of the form, alternates between melodic patterns from the jazz language and rhythmic phrases of varying lengths.

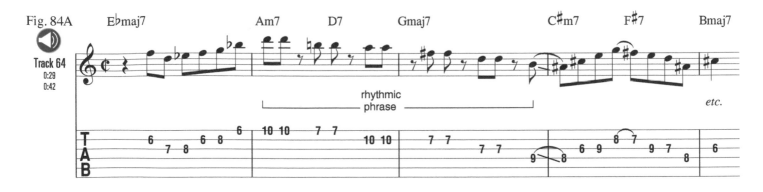

A similar pattern can be used thematically over measures 13–15. The imitated rhythmic motif in **Fig. 84B** produces a question-and-answer phrase structure. Melding the two basic approaches results in a richer improvised line.

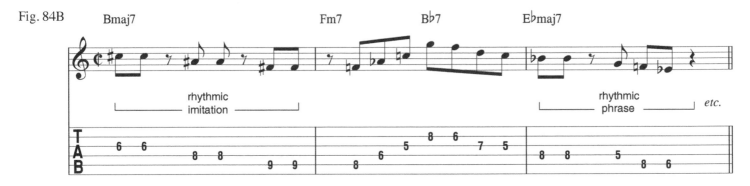

Rhythmic phrasing works well with small melodic fragments. Coltrane used this approach himself to begin his original "alternate-take" solo. In **Fig. 85**, two-note chord partials (major and minor 3rds) are played in staccato patterns over beats 1 and 3 in measures 1–2 and 5–6. These groups are moved horizontally on the fingerboard (linear motion).

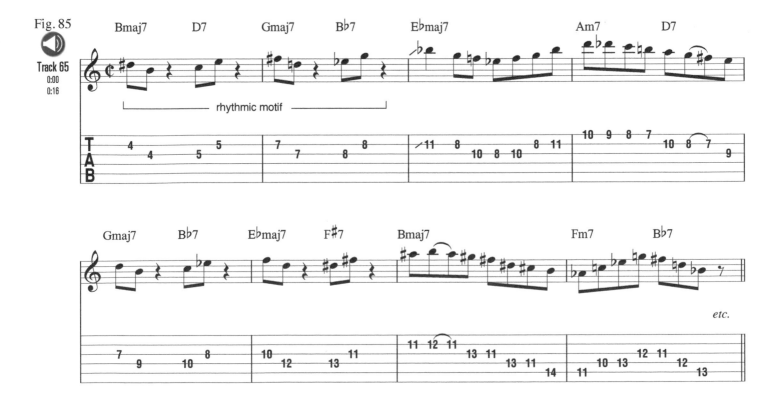

Fig. 86 expounds on the idea of rhythmic phrasing and two-note groups in a more or less fixed position. Note the use of alternating 3rds and 2nds. The rhythmic motif is answered by the bop phrase ending in measure 4.

Consistent eighth-note rhythm, accented three-note scalar groups, and chromatic linear motion converge in **Fig. 87**. The incidental dissonances that occur in the ascending transition from B major to E♭ major are part of the charm and are "legitimized" by the rhythmic forward motion and feeling of arrival in the phrase. This idea comes from Pat Martino, who played patterns like this often in his 1960s work.

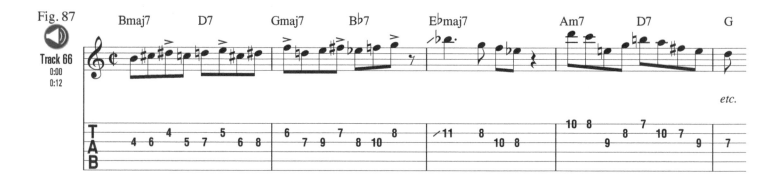

A variation on a theme, **Fig. 88** subjects a three-note chromatic figure to the same procedure. Here we begin on a B–A♯–B "cell" (the tonic and major 7th of B major) and move it up chromatically from B major to E♭ major on a single string. Note the phrasing of two slurred notes and a single picked note in the nuclear pattern. As this cell is moved, rhythmic displacements and shifted rhythms naturally take place.

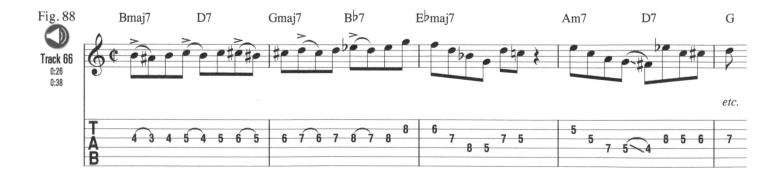

Shorter syncopated figures are effective over the ii–V–I progressions in measures 9–15. **Fig. 89** emphasizes chromatic motion (D#–D–C#) and upper-partial color tones—specifically, the 9ths and augmented 5th (C#m9–F#7#5–Bmaj9).

This variant (**Fig. 90**) exploits a common syncopated rhythm figure favored by Wes Montgomery and John Coltrane, et al. It also emphasizes chromatic motion (G–F#–F) and upper-partial color tones.

Fig. 91 is a longer line that joins three rhythmic phrases of like character. It journeys through three ii–V–I progressions in G major, B major, and E♭ major, respectively. A call-and-response feeling is created by the two phrases in the first four measures. Note the transposition of Fig. 90 to G major in measures 1–2. The phrase in measures 5–6 combines fragments of the two earlier patterns. Note the grafting of Fig. 90 in measure 5 onto the transposed phrase ending of Fig. 89 in measure 6.

II–V–I PROGRESSIONS AND PATTERNS

The ii–V–I is the most common chord progression in jazz. It is found in the blues, "Rhythm" changes, countless standards, and a host of original compositions. Of the latter, "Giant Steps" is definitive. The ii–V–I progression occurs in the transitions of measures 4–5 and 8–9, and utterly dominates the second half of the form, measures 8–16. What makes the ii–V–I patterns so glaringly significant in "Giant Steps" is their usage in defining the motion to and from 3rds-related tonal centers—a central aspect of the tune.

The ii–V–I progressions in "Giant Steps" establish the visited key centers: E♭ major, G major, B major, and E♭ major. Consider the second half of the form. It begins with a ii–V–I pattern in E♭ major: Fm7–B♭7–E♭, measures 8–9. The next two patterns establish G major and B major via Am7–D7–G (measures 10–11) and C♯m7–F♯7–B (measures 12–13), respectively. The key of E♭ major is re-established in measures 14–15 with Fm7–B♭7–E♭. A final abbreviated ii–V progression, C♯m7–F♯7 in 16, functions as a turnaround to the key of B major and another chorus of the changes.

It stands to reason that the advancing player must have a large and workable stockpile of ii–V–I patterns that fit the progressions in "Giant Steps." These are initially accessed and assimilated from the jazz language. They are made practicable through time spent in the woodshed, systematically applying them to tunes. It is absolutely incumbent upon the player to learn and continually update a repertory of ii–V–I figures and patterns. More often than not, the best of these essential licks are gleaned from masters like Charlie Parker, Oscar Peterson, Sonny Rollins, Dexter Gordon, Clifford Brown, Wes Montgomery, and, of course, John Coltrane.

There are generally two types of ii–V–I patterns, distinguished by their time span and harmonic rhythm. The "long" ii–V–I is usually four measures in length. It is played as one measure of ii, one measure of V, and two measures of I. A common variation arranges the progression as one measure of ii–V followed by a second measure of ii–V and then two measures of I.

The "short" ii–V–I compresses the pattern and time span into a two-bar structure: (in 4/4 or 2/2) two beats of ii and two beats of V in measure 1, and four beats of I in measure 2. The harmonic proportions (ratio of ii to V to I) are retained in its shortened form. "Giant Steps" utilizes the short ii–V–I pattern exclusively in measures 8–16 and adaptations of the short pattern in the quick transitions of measures 4–5 and 16–1.

Sources of ii–V–I Patterns

There are three primary sources for suitable ii–V–I patterns to be used in "Giant Steps"— or any other viable tune for that matter. The first, for lack of a better word, is "generic." Generic, often misinterpreted as a pejorative term, here applies specifically to those much-used essential patterns in the genre. They are in such widespread usage that they can be attributed to a large number of artists in the jazz genre. Jazz educators like David Baker, Jerry Coker, Scott Reeves, and Oliver Nelson have written books that codify many of these invaluable patterns.

A second source of ii–V–I patterns comes directly from the master himself via transcriptions of John Coltrane's actual improvised solos in "Giant Steps." Listen to different versions of the tune on the indispensable box set *John Coltrane: The Heavyweight Champion* (Rhino/Atlantic Records) and select your favorites. Then, transcribe your selections or check out extant printed transcriptions. There are a vast number of useful phrases available to players from full transcriptions in publications like David Demsey's *John Coltrane Plays Giant Steps* (Hal Leonard). It is particularly beneficial and enlightening to pore over Coltrane's variations in the numerous alternate takes as well as the master take. Since the transcriptions are written in B♭ (the tenor key, notated a whole step higher than concert pitch), transposition is required, which deepens the learning experience for guitarists.

Another source of ii–V–I patterns comes from personal experience, generally acquired by ear and transcribed from recordings. Learned and assimilated ii–V–I phrases from specific players must be borrowed, repurposed, and applied to the changes at hand. This step is mandatory. It is the way jazz players have learned to play and create since time immemorial.

Every one with a jazz vocabulary has their favorite ii–V–Is. Mine are offered in this section as well. Each is annotated with the artist and the track from which it originated. Sources here include saxophonists Charlie Parker, Sonny Rollins, Dexter Gordon, and Sonny Stitt; trumpeters Dizzy Gillespie and Miles Davis; pianist Hampton Hawes; and guitarists Wes Montgomery, Grant Green, Pat Martino, George Benson, and Tal Farlow. It is vital to transpose each example to the tonal centers in "Giant Steps": Eb major, G major, and B major. Moreover, it is essential to play these patterns in different registers, positions, and fingerings on the guitar.

Generic ii–V–I Patterns

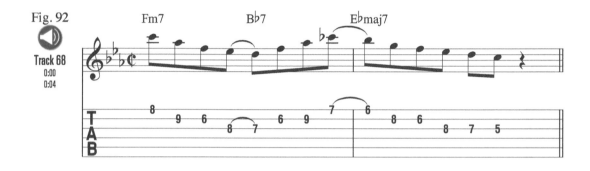

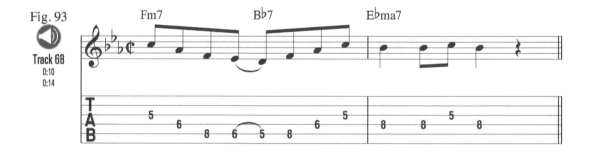

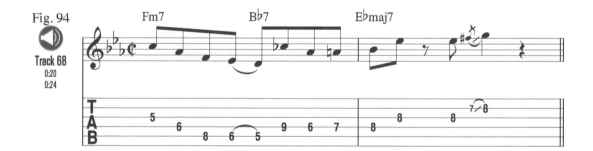

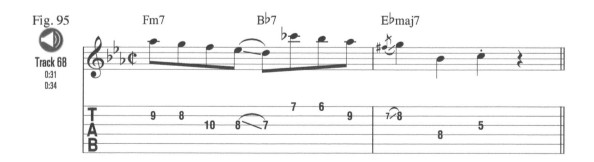

Fig. 96 — Track 68 — 0:41 / 0:44

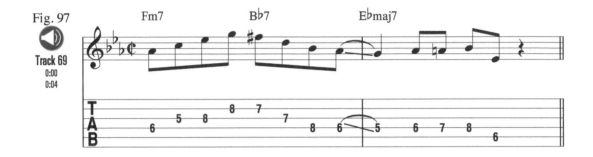

Fig. 97 — Track 69 — 0:00 / 0:04

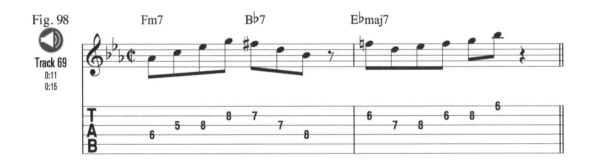

Fig. 98 — Track 69 — 0:11 / 0:15

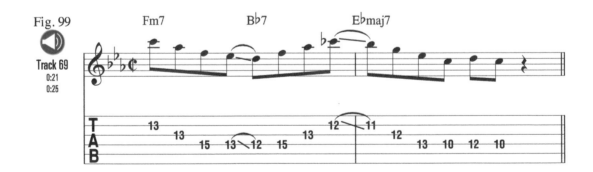

Fig. 99 — Track 69 — 0:21 / 0:25

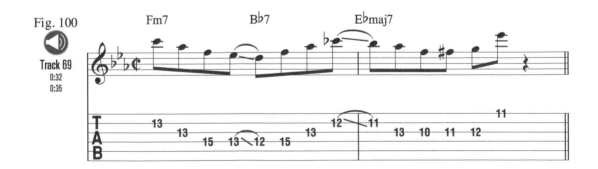

Fig. 100 — Track 69 — 0:32 / 0:35

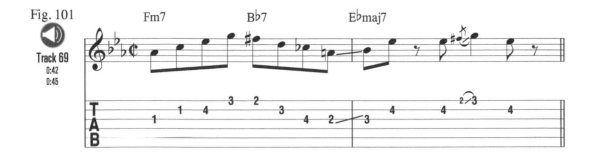

Fig. 101

Track 69
0:42
0:45

Fm7   Bb7   Ebmaj7

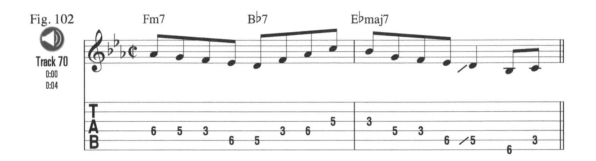

Fig. 102

Track 70
0:00
0:04

Fm7   Bb7   Ebmaj7

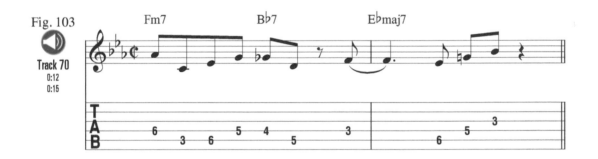

Fig. 103

Track 70
0:12
0:15

Fm7   Bb7   Ebmaj7

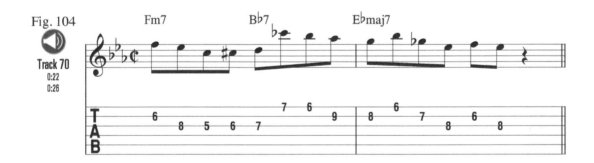

Fig. 104

Track 70
0:22
0:26

Fm7   Bb7   Ebmaj7

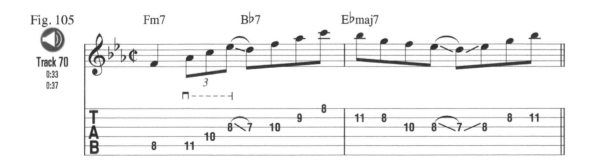

Fig. 105

Track 70
0:33
0:37

Fm7   Bb7   Ebmaj7

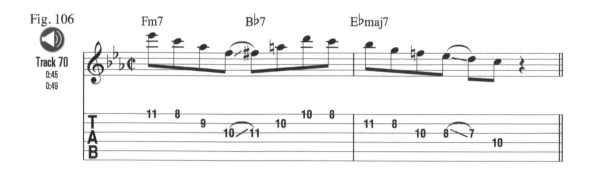

Fig. 106
Track 70
0:45
0:49

Trane ii–V–I Patterns

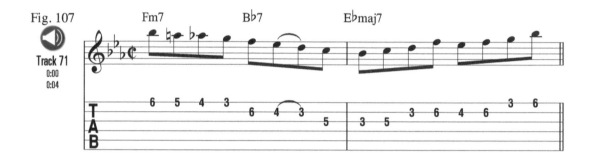

Fig. 107
Track 71
0:00
0:04

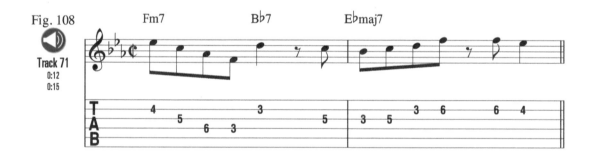

Fig. 108
Track 71
0:12
0:15

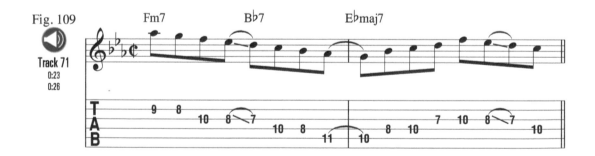

Fig. 109
Track 71
0:23
0:26

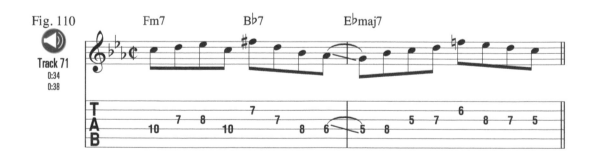

Fig. 110
Track 71
0:34
0:38

Fig. 111

Track 72
0:00
0:04

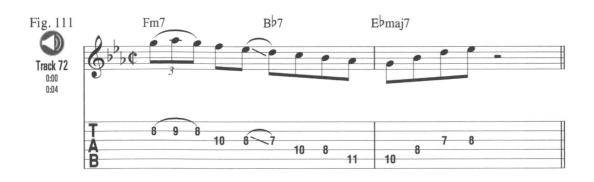

Fig. 112

Track 72
0:10
0:13

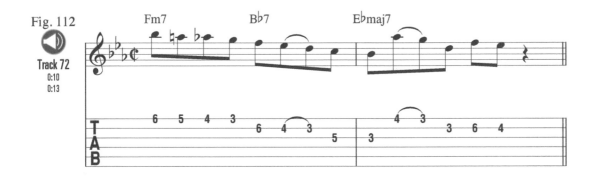

Fig. 113

Track 72
0:21
0:25

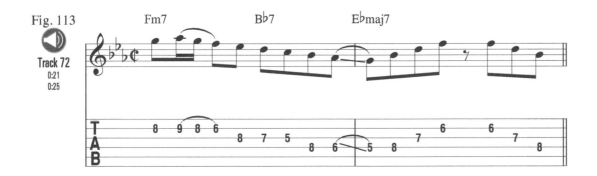

Fig. 114

Track 72
0:33
0:37

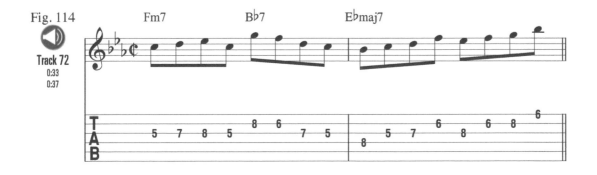

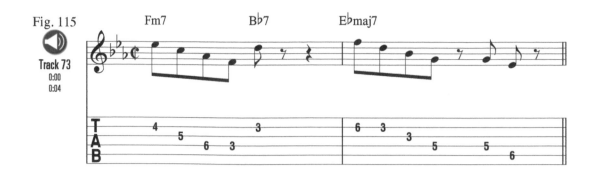

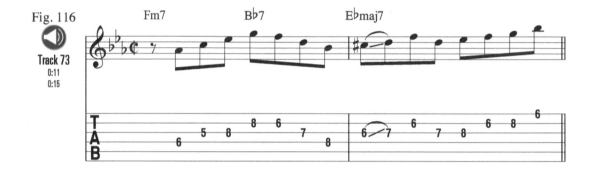

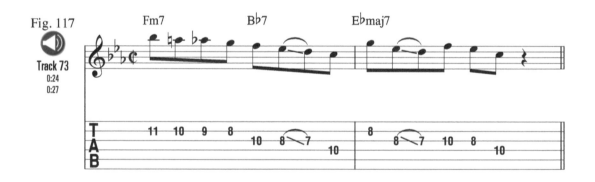

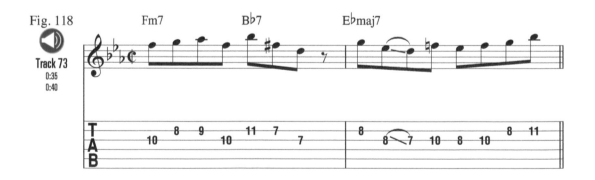

Fig. 119

Track 74
0:00
0:05

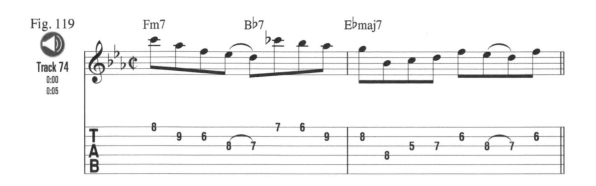

Fig. 120

Track 74
0:14
0:18

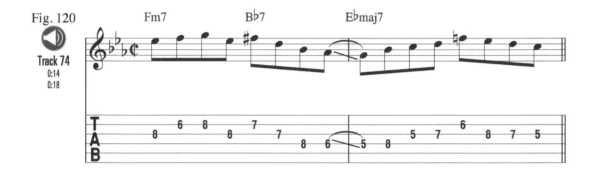

Fig. 121

Track 74
0:27
0:31

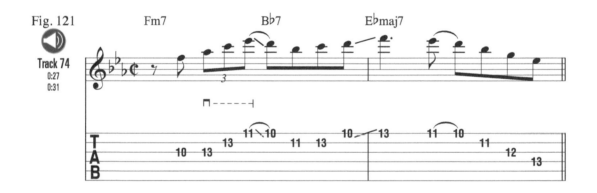

Fig. 122

Track 74
0:39
0:44

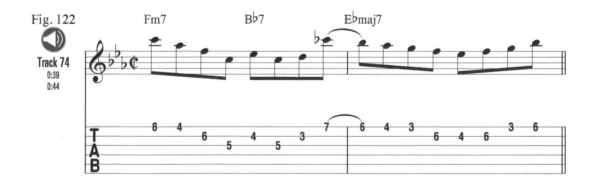

Personal Favorite ii–V–I Patterns

Fig. 123

Charlie Parker: "Donna Lee"

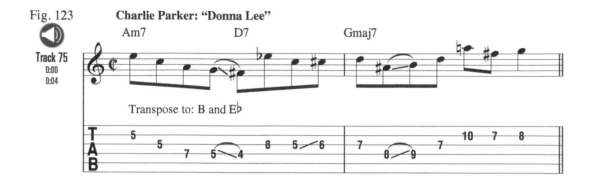

Track 75
0:00
0:04

Fig. 124

Charlie Parker: "Billie's Bounce"

Track 75
0:12
0:16

Fig. 125

Dizzy Gillespie: "Anthropology"

Track 75
0:22
0:26

Fig. 126

Miles Davis: "Airegin"

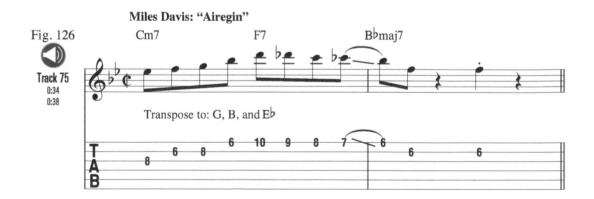

Track 75
0:34
0:38

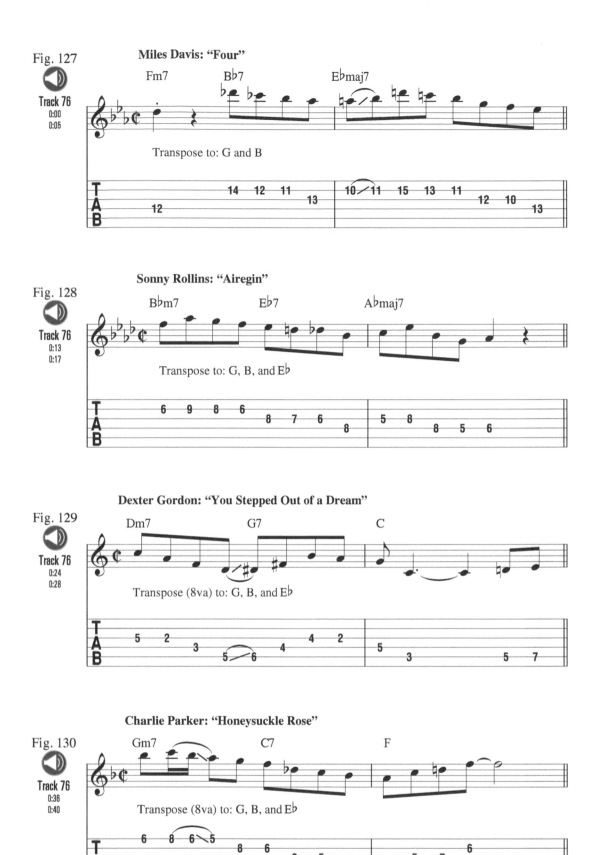

Fig. 127

Track 76
0:00
0:05

Miles Davis: "Four"

Transpose to: G and B

Fig. 128

Track 76
0:13
0:17

Sonny Rollins: "Airegin"

Transpose to: G, B, and E♭

Fig. 129

Track 76
0:24
0:28

Dexter Gordon: "You Stepped Out of a Dream"

Transpose (8va) to: G, B, and E♭

Fig. 130

Track 76
0:36
0:40

Charlie Parker: "Honeysuckle Rose"

Transpose (8va) to: G, B, and E♭

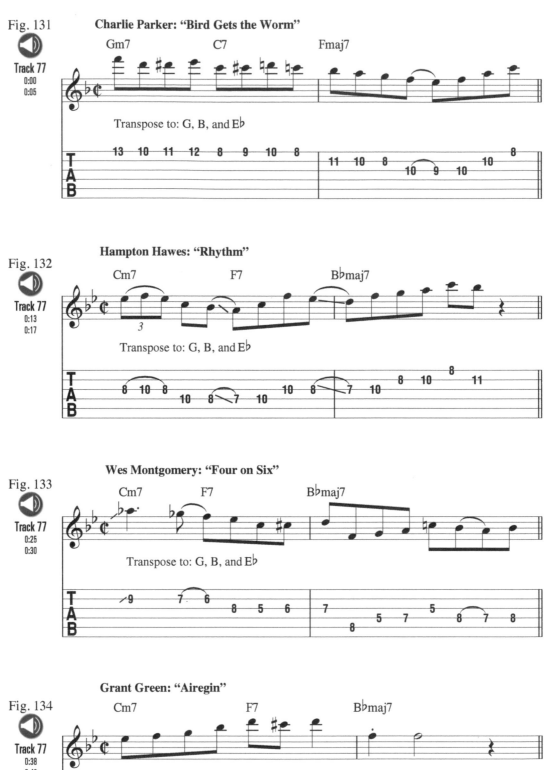

Charlie Parker: "Bird Gets the Worm"

Fig. 131

Track 77
0:00
0:05

Transpose to: G, B, and E♭

Hampton Hawes: "Rhythm"

Fig. 132

Track 77
0:13
0:17

Transpose to: G, B, and E♭

Wes Montgomery: "Four on Six"

Fig. 133

Track 77
0:25
0:30

Transpose to: G, B, and E♭

Grant Green: "Airegin"

Fig. 134

Track 77
0:38
0:42

Transpose to: G, B, and E♭

Fig. 135

Track 78
0:00
0:04

Pat Martino: "Airegin"

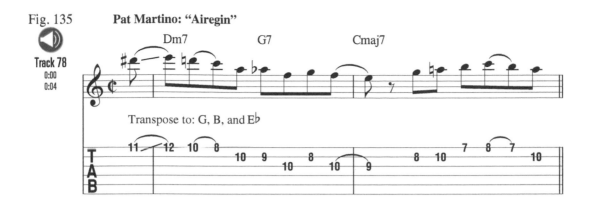

Transpose to: G, B, and E♭

Fig. 136

Track 78
0:13
0:17

George Benson: "Billie's Bounce"

Transpose to: G, B, and E♭

Fig. 137

Track 78
0:25
0:29

Tal Farlow: "St. Thomas"

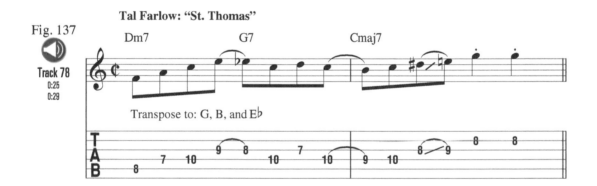

Transpose to: G, B, and E♭

Fig. 138

Track 78
0:37
0:41

Sonny Stitt: "52nd St. Theme"

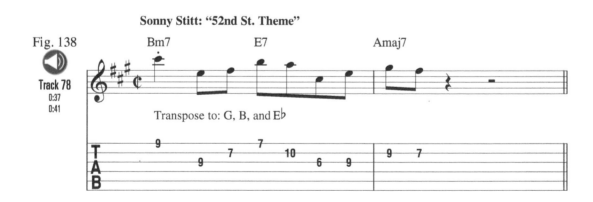

Transpose to: G, B, and E♭

Working with ii–V–I Patterns and Progressions

Once a collection of ii–V–I phrases is in your grasp, the fun really begins. Practice any combination of your favorite patterns over the "Giant Steps" changes in measures 8–16. This procedure builds the foundation for meaningful improvisations with materials to which you are personally attracted. Here are a few examples of ii–V–I patterns played over discrete four-bar segments of "Giant Steps" changes. These phrases employ various combinations of generic patterns, Trane patterns, and personal favorite ii–V–I patterns.

Some Basic ii–V–I Patterns

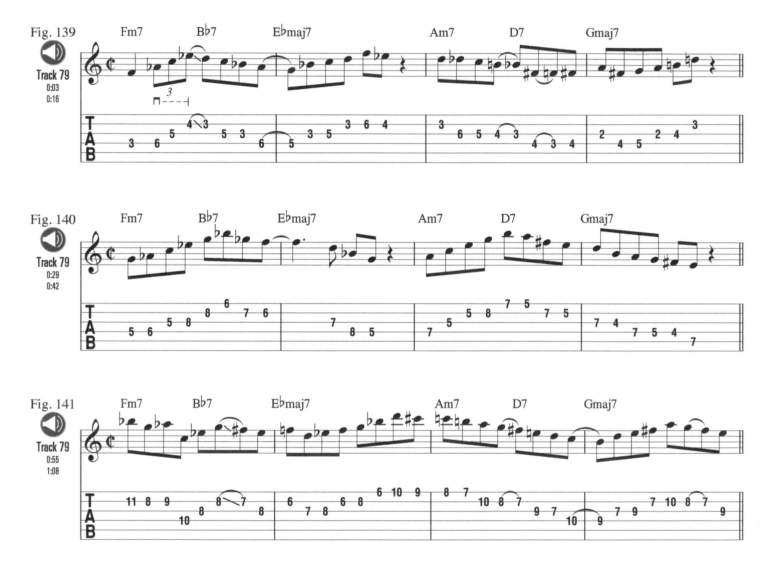

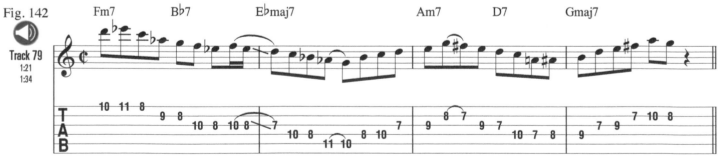

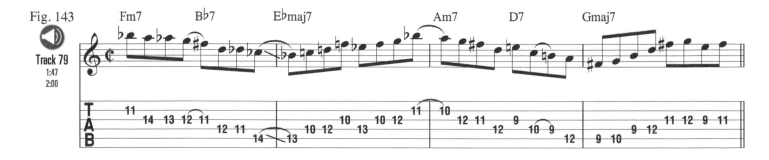

Fig. 143
Track 79
1:47
2:00

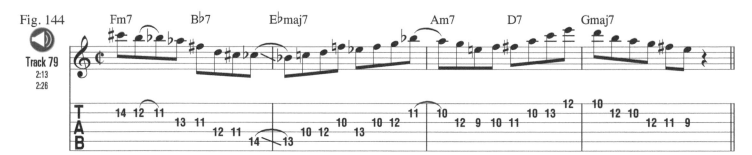

Fig. 144
Track 79
2:13
2:26

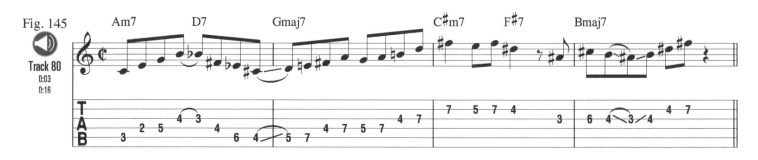

Fig. 145
Track 80
0:03
0:16

Fig. 146
Track 80
0:28
0:42

Fig. 147
Track 80
0:54
1:08

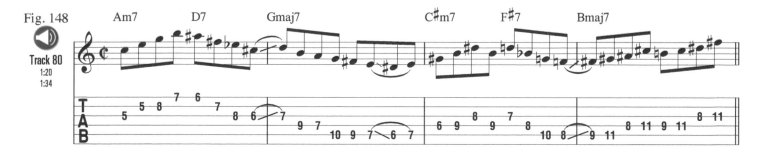

Fig. 148
Track 80
1:20
1:34

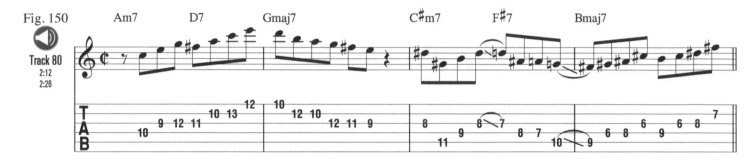

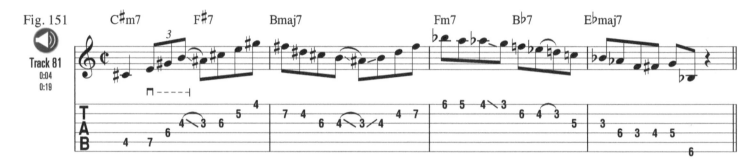

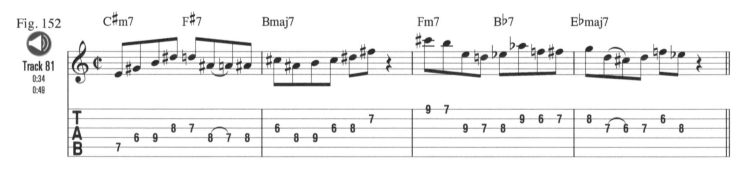

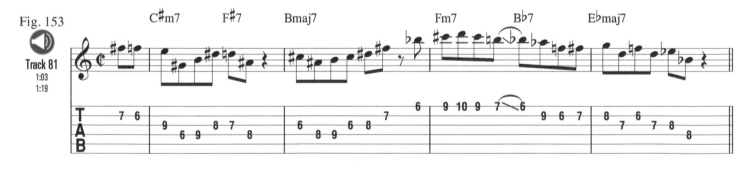

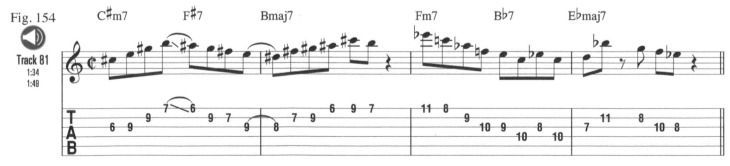

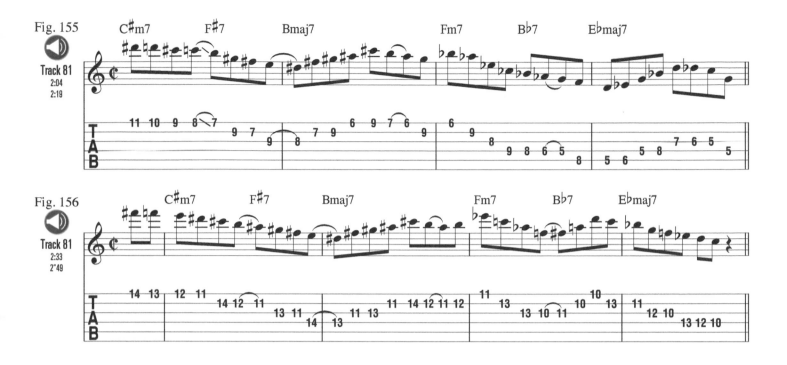

Three Additional Phrases

Here are three additional phrases that illustrate a midway destination point to be reached as a practice goal. In these examples, two linked ii–V–I patterns rotate forward in 3rds-related cycles, as in the second half of the "Giant Steps" song form.

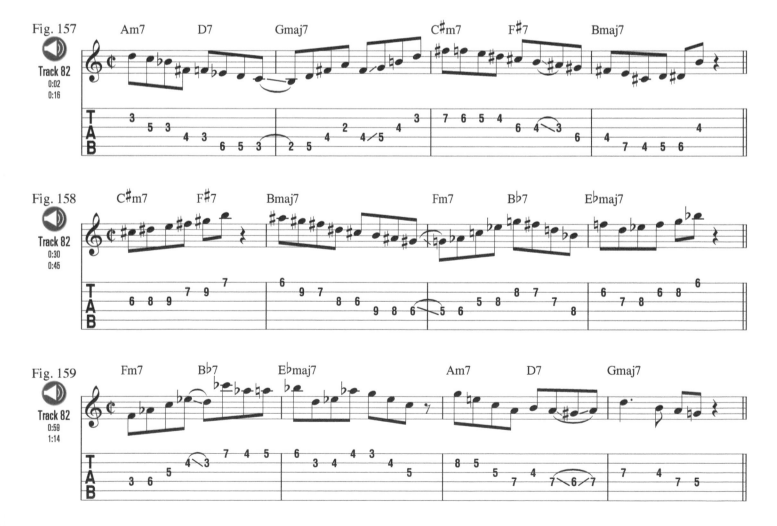

A Thematic Approach to the ii–V–Is in "Giant Steps"

Thematic approaches work well over the cycles of ii–V–Is in measures 8–16 of "Giant Steps." They provide musical contrast and variety within improvisation and an alternative to pattern-oriented lines. Moreover, they convey a sense of large-scale melodic activity. We have seen the effect of applying largely rhythmic concepts to the changes in an earlier section (see "Rhythmic Approaches"). Thematic approaches offer another solution to the challenges of "Giant Steps."

The next two examples illustrate the introduction and variation of motifs through 3rds-related changes. Note the use of contour imitation, melodic repetition, and sequencing of ii–V–I melodies in both examples. Chromatic connections, such as C to B in the linking of E♭maj7 to Am7, and D to D♯ in the linking of Gmaj7 to C♯m7, are emphasized in **Fig. 160**.

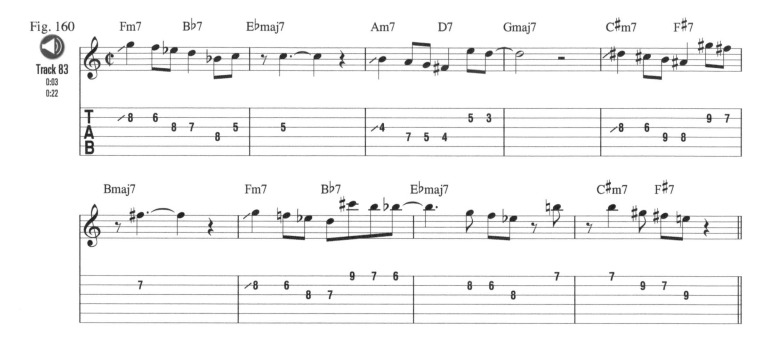

Fig. 160

Fig. 161 exploits a gradually rising sequence in which each new ii–V–I pattern ascends to the nearest related chord tone of the next pattern in a new tonal center. For instance, B♭ begins the first ii–V–I (Fm7–B♭7–E♭maj7) and leads to B, which begins the next ii–V–I (Am7–D7–Gmaj7). Note the deliberate wide interval leaps in the melodies. The idea is to apply a steady stepwise climb until D♯ is reached in the final ii–V (C♯m7–F♯7). In the process, color tones such as the 9th, 11th, and 13th are highlighted.

Fig. 161

What goes up must come down. Here's another thematic possibility. In **Fig. 162**, a descending sequence approach is pursued with each pattern unit. Note the large-scale melodic motion (B♭–A–G♯–G): B♭ (to begin Fm7 on the 11th tone) to A (to begin Am7 on the tonic) to G♯ (to begin C♯m7 on the 5th), and finally to G (to begin Fm7 on the 9th). The idea is to express the ii–V–I changes as a chromatic line with each tone on beat 1 of measures 1, 3, 5, and 7, representing a significant chord note in a new key center. No two patterns are alike and, indeed, each has an individual melodic character, but they share a similar phrase feeling. The last two notes of E♭maj7, in measures 2 and 8 of this example, are the same pitches an octave apart and are linked to a typical jazz figure.

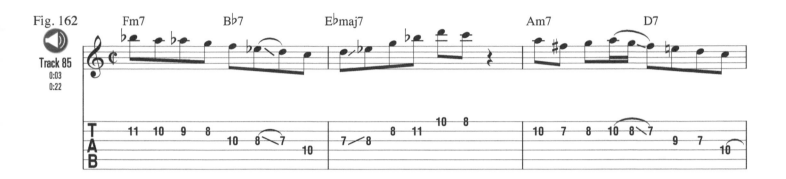

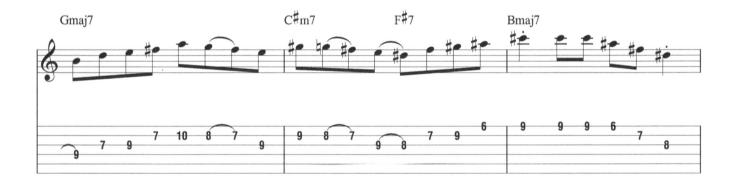

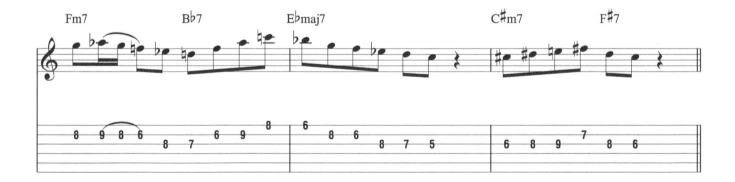

MODEL SOLOS

As a performer becomes more confident, fluent, and technically proficient at playing the essential patterns and phrases, every effort should be made to introduce melodies from modern jazz—specifically the bebop language—into "Giant Steps." One excellent method for mining the core vocabulary and facilitating this part of the necessary skill sets is to create model solos.

A model solo is a precomposed chorus in which material for improvisation is worked out, and often written out, ahead of time. In making model solos, the player accesses and incorporates elements from their own repertory—their personal pool of licks. These are selected, then brought into context and subjected to usage. Here's where the Trane patterns meet your acquired licks from Charlie Parker, Clifford Brown, Oscar Peterson, Joe Pass, Wes Montgomery, Dexter Gordon, Hampton Hawes, and Pat Martino—or whomever you admire.

All right, you have the basic patterns under your fingers. You've accumulated and gotten comfortable with the components. You have some favorite ii–V–I phrases, some rhythmic concepts, some common-tone figures, a handful of melodic themes, and you understand how to hook them together. What's next? Let's build a model solo.

A model solo is a work in progress, a starting point in your evolving improvisational adventure. Model solos act like springboards for future extemporaneous playing. Building a model solo for "Giant Steps" involves a balance of worked-out pattern material and elements of the core jazz language. More specifically, use basic training patterns and phrases for the two 3rds-related progressions in the first eight measures, and then apply your favorite ii–V–I melodies to the remainder of the form. Initially, the latter may be culled from the chapter on ii–V–Is in "Giant Steps."

Constructing a Model Solo

Constructing a model solo requires a basic strategy and a few simple preliminary steps. First, determine where you are going, and where you will place the various patterns and licks you have assimilated and practiced. This chord chart depicts the entire 16-bar form (one chorus) of "Giant Steps." Consider this chart a roadmap and template for future improvisations.

Fig. 163

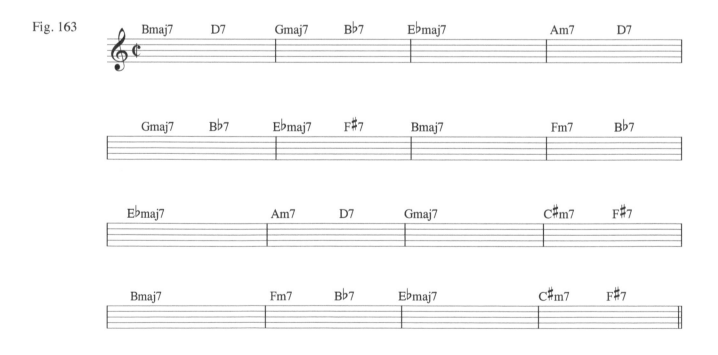

When constructing a model solo, it is useful at the outset to divide the form into logical sections. The first four-bar section (measures 1–4) is the starting point for applying the 49 basic patterns established in "Basic Trane-ing."

Fig. 164

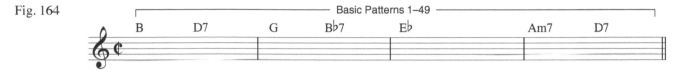

Here's the next section. The second four-bar section (measures 5–8) is where you will use transposed versions of the 49 basic patterns, now beginning on the G major chord. Make a conscious effort to link transposed phrases. These should flow logically from preceding material in measure 4 (Am7–D7). In time, you will create your variations and connections of the basic patterns on the fly.

Fig. 165

The next section addresses the large part of the form. This section contains four longer two-bar phrases, made of ii–V–I progressions in Eb major, G major, B major, and Eb major respectively. Here, you will select and apply the ii–V–I patterns from the previous chapter, or your own favorite melodies.

Fig. 166

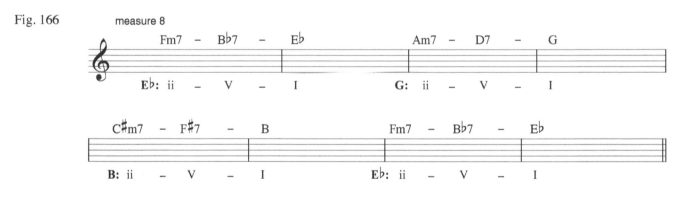

Turnarounds

The final measure of the 16-bar form can be perceived in two basic ways. First, it can be seen as the formal end of the chorus, in which a phrase actually ends and acts as a period. Second, it can be played as a short turnaround, in which a one-bar pickup line over C#m7–F#7 leads to the next chorus and the beginning of a new pattern on B.

Fig. 167

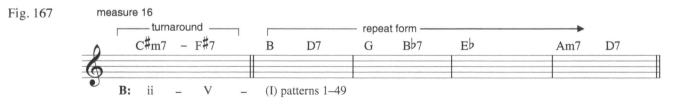

These turnaround phrases present several options for the last measure of the "Giant Steps" form (C#m7–F#7). They demonstrate the linking of a pickup line with a basic pattern (beginning on B major) for a new chorus. The three examples depict approaches to basic patterns 1–3. Note the use of A# as a leading tone to B, defining the move from F#7 to B major.

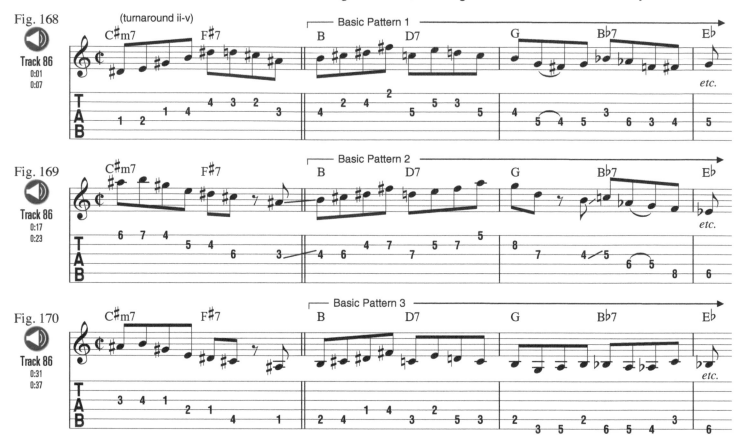

A basic pattern can be approached with a variety of turnarounds. Here, three distinct sounds are used over C#m7–F#7. The first (**Fig. 171A**) is a chromatic line and an F# augmented arpeggio (F#–D–A#). The second (**Fig. 171B**) is a diminished scale melody and an F# augmented arpeggio. The third (**Fig. 171C**) is a diatonic line and an F# augmented arpeggio. These three pickup lines of differing character are linked to basic pattern #4.

A turnaround figure may incorporate pieces of the bebop language. This ii–V lick has telltale elements of Charlie Parker and Wes Montgomery, and is linked to basic pattern #5.

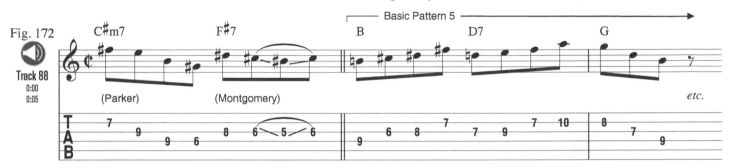

An effective turnaround should address its melodic destination. Put simply, it must turn around and go somewhere. In "Giant Steps," that specifically means the transition from measure 16 (C#m7–F#7) to measure 1 of a new chorus (B major). This ii–V–I lick (**Fig. 173**) contains chromaticism and a descending F# augmented arpeggio (D–A#–F#) that anticipates a pattern starting on the 9th (C#) of B major. The C# tone is the goal of the turnaround and approached by an upward leap.

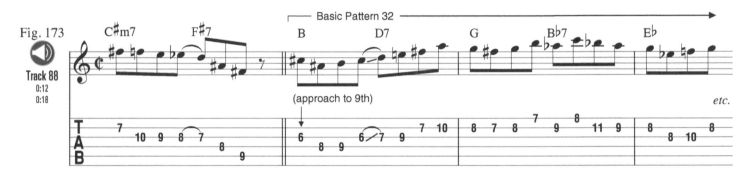

Fig. 174 is a variant of the last phrase. It contains a strong passing tone E that demands resolution to D#, the 3rd of B major. Here, the E–D# melodic approach figure boils down the harmonic action in the F#7 to B chord change, and tags it onto an F# augmented arpeggio.

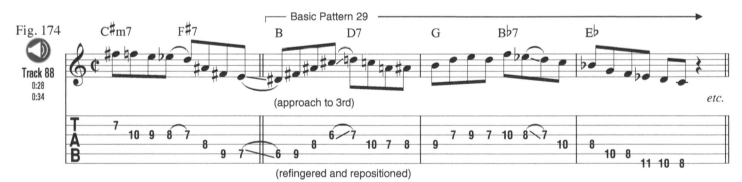

The bebop scale is an indispensable tool that spells out a ii–V change with clarity and musical authenticity. In **Fig. 175**, the bebop scale appears in a typical stepwise descent and leads to F#, the 5th of a B major chord.

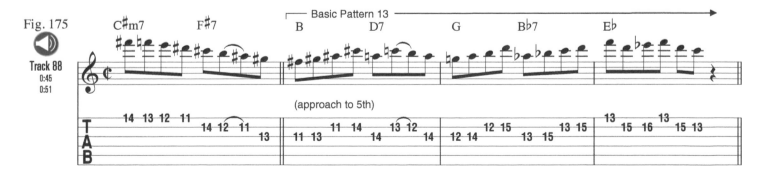

Four Model Solos

The following choruses are offered to the advancing guitarist as examples of model solos for "Giant Steps." Each solo is played over one chorus of the 16-bar form. A brief summary and analysis of the patterns and elements of the applied jazz language is included.

Model Solo 1

Measures 1–4:	Basic pattern #1.
Measures 5–8:	Basic pattern #16 transposed to G.
Measure 9:	A major-blues chromatic lick.
Measures 10 & 11:	A favorite Charlie Parker ii–V–I.
Measures 12 & 13:	Bebop arpeggio outlines and a hexatonic phrase ending.
Measures 14 & 15:	A favorite Dexter Gordon line and hexatonic melody with neighbor-tone figure.
Measure 16:	A classic bop minor-mode lick.

Model Solo 2

Fig. 177
Track 90
0:00
0:24

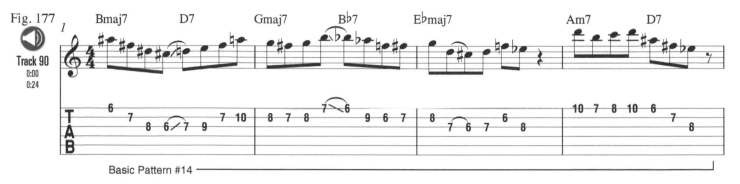

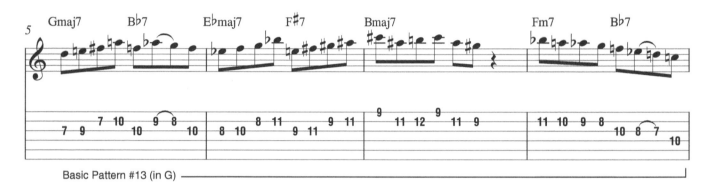

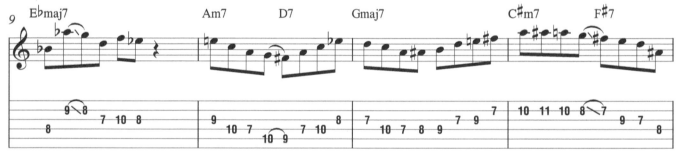

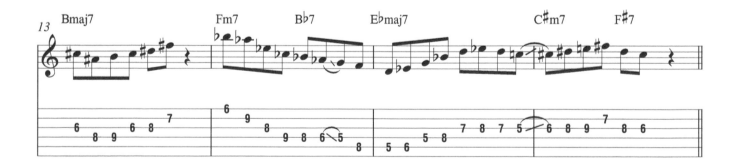

Measures 1–4:	Basic pattern #14.
Measures 5–8:	Basic pattern #13 transposed to begin on G.
Measure 9:	A must-know Coltrane melody.
Measures 10 & 11:	Bebop arpeggio outlining a bop voice-leading figure and hexatonic phrase ending.
Measures 12 & 13:	A diminished/augmented lick borrowed from Howard Roberts grafted onto a Pat Martino phrase ending.
Measures 14 & 15:	A Joe Pass descent answered by a Charlie Parker ascent. Note the use of a "plural scale" in this and the last phrase. Notes used over Fm7–B♭7 retained from B major function as an altered-scale sound.
Measure 16:	The bop minor-mode lick from the previous chorus played an octave higher.

Model Solo 3

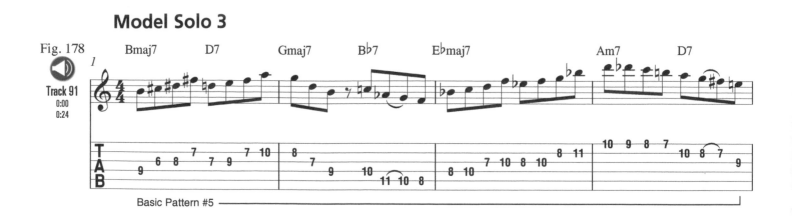

Measures 1–4:	Basic pattern #5.
Measures 5–7:	Basic pattern #13 (partial form), transposed to begin on G with a varied phrase ending.
Measure 8 & 9:	A thematic ii–V–I line in E♭ begins a sequential approach to the changes.
Measures 10 & 11:	The thematic line imitated and varied in G.
Measures 12 & 13:	A contrasting melody with a bebop voice-leading pattern, borrowed from Charlie Parker.
Measures 14 & 15:	Elements of the earlier line in E♭ embellished with chromatic tones. The phrase ending is a classic hexatonic lick.
Measure 16:	The phrase ending in E♭ moved a half step higher functions as a transposed ii–V line over C♯m7–F♯7. This is an important strategy to apply in the final two measures of the "Giant Steps" changes.

Model Solo 4

Track 92
0:00
0:24

Fig. 179

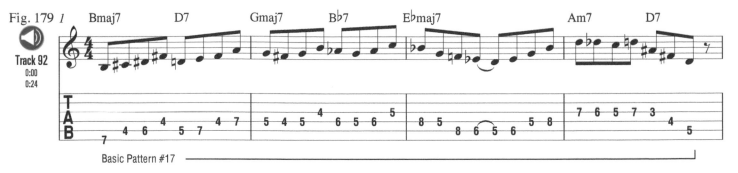

Basic Pattern #17

Basic Pattern #16 — #8 — #8 — #43 — #14

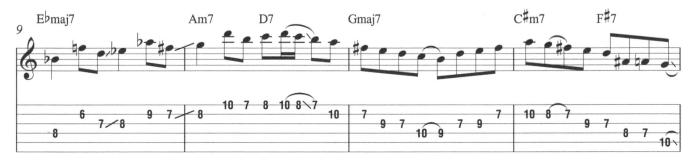

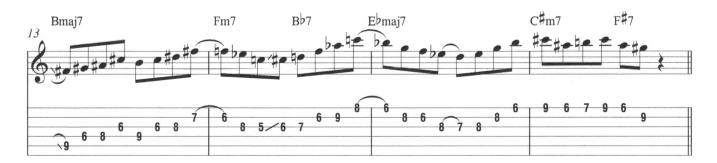

Measures 1–4:	Basic pattern #17.
Measures 5–8:	Fragmentation and transposition at work. Measure 5 is a fragment of pattern #16 over Gmaj7–B♭7, measure 6 is a fragment of pattern #8 in two contexts over E♭maj7–F♯7, measure 7 is a short hexatonic figure, and measure 8 is a fragment of #14 over Fm7–B♭7.
Measure 9–10:	A zigzagging line borrowed from Joe Pass, connecting E♭ and Am7 chords with the common tone G. The fragment of #15 is varied and played over Am7 and D7.
Measure 11:	A largely hexatonic melody in G emphasizing the 7th and 6h tones, F♯ and E.
Measure 12:	The G sound held over as a "plural scale" leads to an altered-scale resolution to B. Note the half-step approach: G to F♯.
Measure 13:	Two four-note Trane cycle patterns over B major, 5–6–7–2 (F♯–G♯–A♯–C♯) and 1–2–3–5 (B–C♯–D♯–F♯). This is a classic I chord figure in the jazz language.
Measures 14–15:	A bop voice-leading figure and B♭9 arpeggio lead to a hexatonic line in E♭.
Measure 16:	A recall and imitation of the fragment in measure 8, here over C♯m7–F♯7.
Overall:	Note the long string of eighth notes in measures 10–16 and half-step approaches to B (G–F♯) and Fm7 (F♯–F) chords.

Constructing a Model Solo with Specific Motifs

At some point in the process of constructing model solos, it is imperative to consciously apply new material from the jazz repertory. Let's explore one case. Imagine we have selected a specific figure—call it a motif or lick—to be applied to the "Giant Steps" changes. This motif is a standard theme of the bebop language, transcribed directly from one of Charlie Parker's improvised solos. It has been affectionately called the "honey lick" because of its similarity to a prevailing melody in the well-known standard "Honeysuckle Rose."

There are generally two forms of the "honey lick." Here, they are labeled 1A and 1B and shown as part of a two-bar phrase resolving to G major. However, the "honey lick" in this context is transposed and functions as a *tritone substitution*. Normally played a flatted 5th (tritone) away over D7, it is applied as an A♭7 sound resolving a half step down to G major. This yields a more dissonant formula and arguably a more modern expression of a common jazz melody. When applied to the ii–V changes in "Giant Steps," the transposed motif takes on an urgent post-bop quality demanding resolution. As such, it offers a distinct melodic alternative to other procedures typically followed in improvising over the tune.

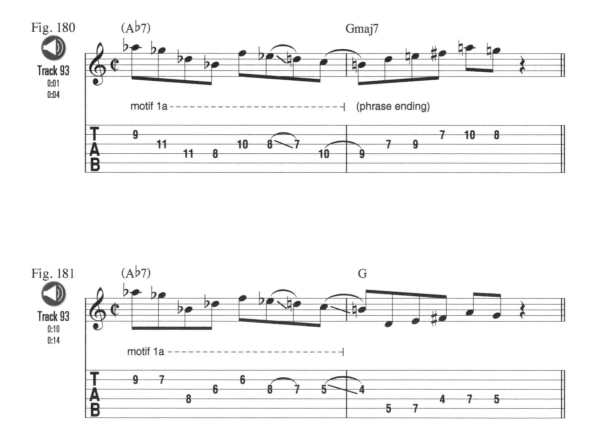

This model solo is an example of the "drop in" method of motivic development. Here, every ii–V progression receives a version of motif 1A or 1B. That's the basic formula at work in this model solo. Each formula is systematically applied to the tonal centers of G major (measures 4–5), E♭ major (8–9), G major (10–11), B major (12–13), and E♭ major (14–15). The model solo utilizes elements of the basic patterns (labeled in the music) in measures 1–8, expanded by motifs 1A and 1B. In measures 8–15, motifs 1A or 1B are "dropped in" to the ii–V sections of the changes. Caveat: This demonstration example intentionally overuses the "drop in" for every applicable part of the progression, as a means to an end. In normal improvising, a more judicious use of "dropped in" motifs is preferable.

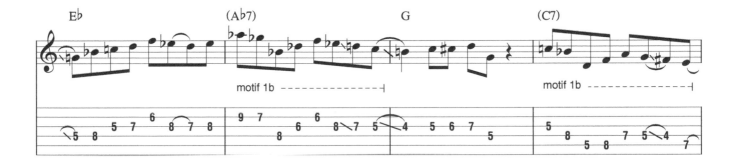

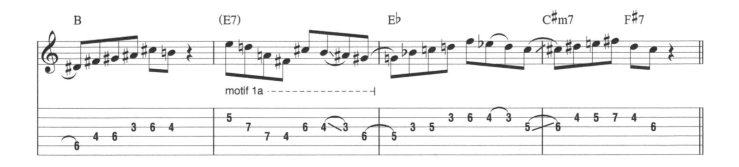

The following two audio accompaniment tracks take place over one chorus of the 16-bar form in "Giant Steps." (Refer to Fig. 163 for a chart of the changes.) They are offered as a starting point for you to create your own model solos. There are two renditions in this section. The first is played at a fast tempo and the second at a slower tempo. Use these tracks as blank templates for your ongoing experiments on "Giant Steps."

Fast Accompaniment Track

Track 95

Moderate Accompaniment Track

Track 96

After exploring and getting familiar with a single 16-bar chorus, take it to the next level. Play combinations of your favorite sounds over a multi-chorus form. This extended improvised solo (**Fig. 183**) stands as an example of an eight-chorus "Giant Steps." It is transcribed and notated and offered as one possible improvisation. However, I have made a concerted effort to intentionally place in context many of the concepts and sounds from previous chapters. Note the use of patterns galore, various ii–V–I figures of mixed origins, rhythmic and thematic approaches, and other ideas. It is followed by an eight-chorus accompaniment track over which you may try your hand at soloing on "Giant Steps."

—Wolf Marshall

Wolf Marshall's Improvised Solo

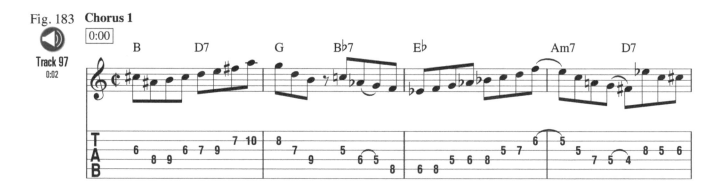

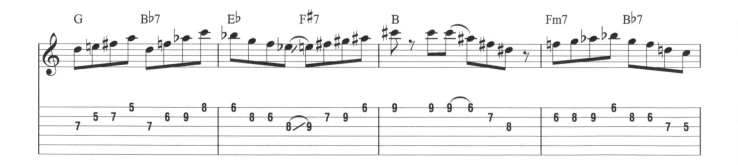

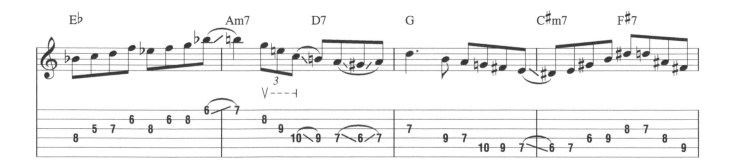

Chorus 2

0:19

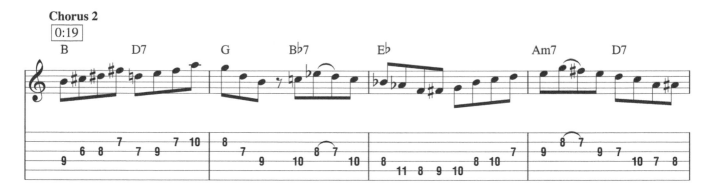

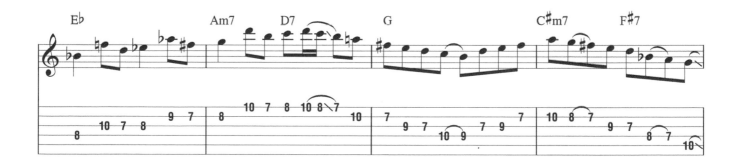

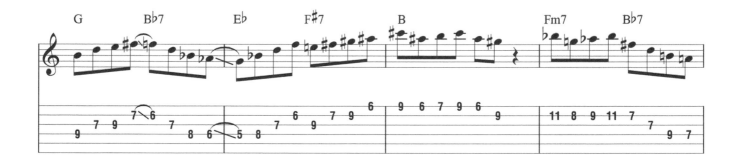

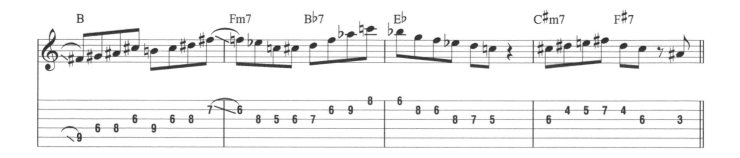

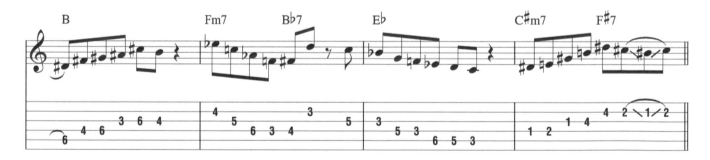

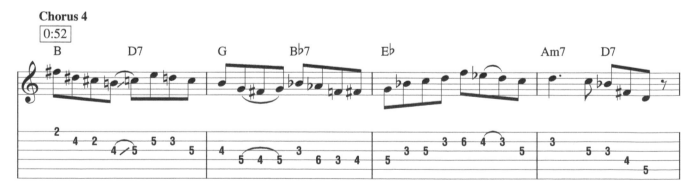

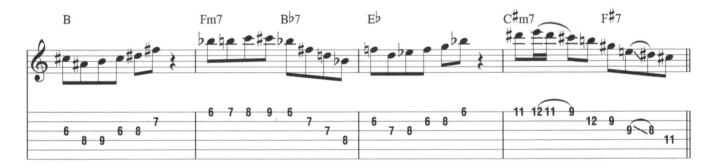

Chorus 5
1:09

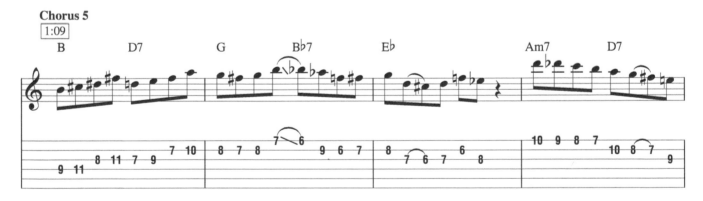

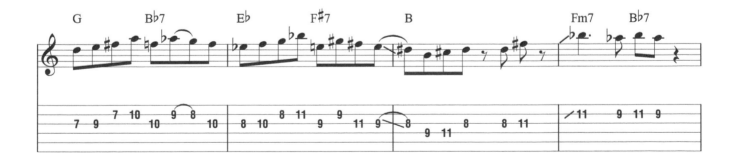

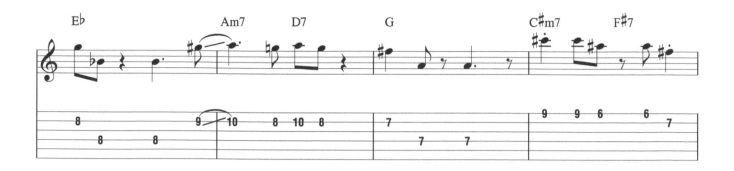

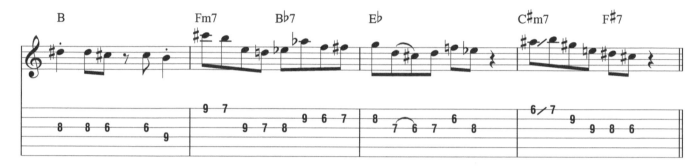

Chorus 6

1:26

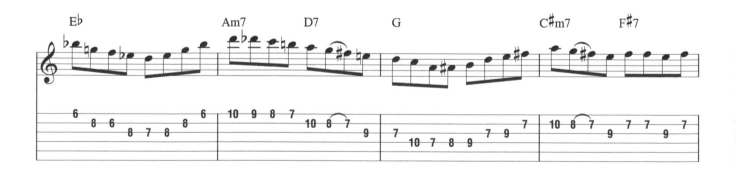

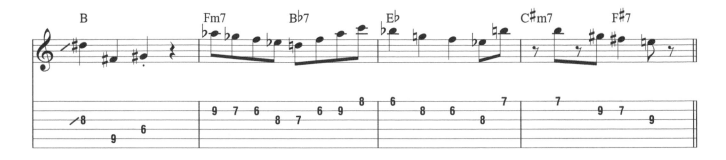

Chorus 7

1:42

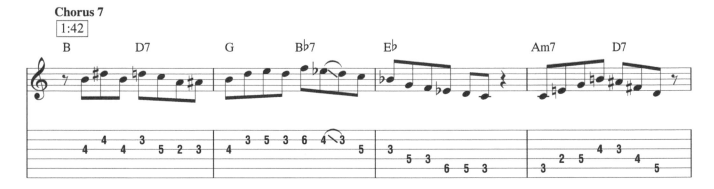

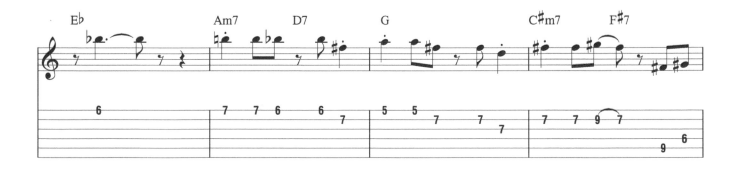

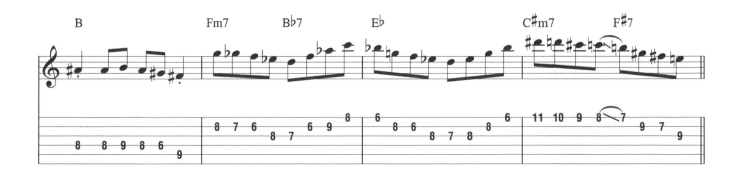

Chorus 8

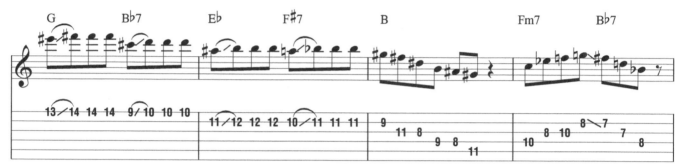

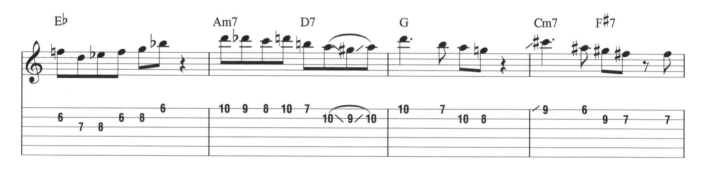

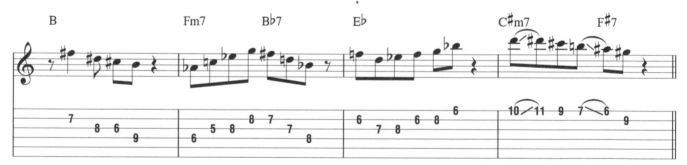

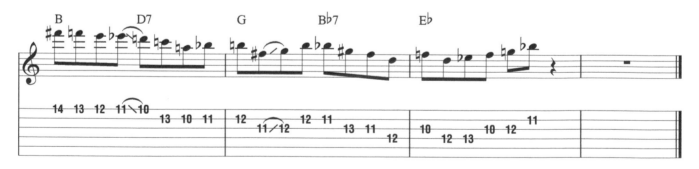

Eight-Chorus Accompaniment Track

Track 98